SHABBAT SHALOM

BY SUSAN R. FRIEDLAND

Ribs

Caviar

The Passover Table

The Jewish American Kitchen
by Raymond Sokolov (recipes)

Susan R. Friedland

LITTLE, BROWN AND COMPANY

Boston   New York   London

SHABBAT
SHALOM

RECIPES AND MENUS
FOR THE SABBATH

FIRST EDITION

Library of Congress Cataloging-in-Publication Data
Friedland, Susan R.
    Shabbat shalom : recipes and menus for the
sabbath / Susan R. Friedland.— 1st ed.
        p.   cm.
    Includes bibliographical references and index.
    ISBN 0-316-29065-3
    1. Cookery, Jewish. 2. Sabbath.   I. Title.
TX724.F688   1999
641.5'676 — dc21   99-35684
                                           CIP

10 9 8 7 6 5 4 3 2 1

MV-NY

Book design by Anne Chalmers

Printed in the United States of America

DEDICATED TO

THE MEMORIES OF MY MOTHER,
BERTHA GROSSMAN,

AND MY SISTER,
CORINNE SCHUBE

I shall never forget Shabbat in my town. When I shall have forgotten everything else, my memory will still retain the atmosphere of holiday, of serenity pervading even the poorest houses; the white tablecloth, the candles, the meticulously combed little girls, the men on the way to the synagogue. When my town shall fade into the abyss of time, I will continue to remember the light and the warmth it radiated on Shabbat.

The jealousies and grudges, the petty rancors between neighbors could wait. As could the debts and worries, the danger. Everything could wait. As it enveloped the universe, the Shabbat conferred on it a dimension of peace, an aura of love.

ELIE WIESEL, *A Jew Today*

CONTENTS

ACKNOWLEDGMENTS

I am grateful to many people for their help and encouragement: Carla Mayer Glasser, the agent for this book, for coming to me with the excellent idea of writing a book on Friday-night dinner. Ronni Stolzenberg, who, in an instant, came up with the right title. Gale Robinson, for her long and precise memory, excellent recipes, and facility for composing menus. Arthur Schwartz, for cooking with me and always having the answer or at least an interesting speculation. Rabbi Harlan Wechsler, who with intelligence and sensitivity read the introduction. Karen Selig took me on explorations of kosher markets in Brooklyn and offered guidance. Letty Cottin Pogrebin lent me two precious books. Mary Rodgers of Cuisinart supplied me with an ice-cream maker. Many other people helped with suggestions and recipes, and they are identified throughout the book. Rick Kot, my friend and the editor of this book, has offered sound advice and generously accommodated my postponements. I am grateful for his confidence and his good company.

SHABBAT SHALOM

INTRODUCTION

Remember the Sabbath day to keep it holy.
Six days shall you labor, and do all your work;
but the seventh day is a Sabbath unto the
Lord your God, in it you shall not do any
manner of work, you, nor thy maid-servant,
man-servant, nor thy cattle, nor thy stranger
that is within thy gates; for in six days the
Lord made heaven and earth, the sea, and all
that in them is, and rested on the seventh day;
wherefore the Lord blessed the Sabbath day,
and hallowed it.

EXODUS 20:8–11

When I was a girl, waybackwhen, the rhythm of the household was determined by the Jewish holidays. There was enormous bustle and disruption around Passover and a lot of talk about it before we actually started shifting dishes around, cleaning the house, and "selling" the chometz. It seemed to me that Passover preparation started at Purim, thirty days before the first seder. Rosh Hashanah was much easier. It meant long walks back and forth to synagogue, in my best new clothes (and shoes that always hurt my feet), and then lunch at our house or at one of my aunts'. Yom Kippur was a very serious matter, but no food preparations were required other than the pre–Kol Nidre meal, which wasn't much of a meal anyway. Break fast was always a much-anticipated opportunity to enjoy dairy, but it mainly featured store-bought smoked fish and a noodle pudding made well in advance. We always went to synagogue for Sukkoth and Shavuoth (a holiday we loved, for it meant my mother's superb blintzes), but there wasn't too much household drama surrounding these festivals.

But Shabbos! Shabbos occurred every

single week, punctuating our lives in a way that undoubtedly established our Jewish identity, not only to ourselves, the children in the family, but to our neighbors, Jews as well as non-Jews. The weekly rituals, the reverence I observed in the adults, created a rich and powerful context for Jewish life. (I call the day Shabbos, the Yiddish word for Sabbath, because that's the way we always referred to it. *Shabbat* is the Hebrew word, and I have to think a second before I use it.)

Every Friday an aura surrounded the household that clearly signaled my mother was up to something serious, and I had to be, too. The morning saw her in a flurry of preparation — soup, kugel, maybe a green vegetable, a chicken for roasting, a compote, or maybe a gelatin dessert with canned fruit suspended in it. No matter what else she was doing, no matter where she was, to the end of her very long life, fifteen to twenty minutes before sundown my mother lit candles. She warned me, as her mother had warned her, that once the moment had passed, it was better not to light them at all because it is prohibited to light a flame on Shabbat. The respect for the day was also reflected in the white tablecloth and the linen or damask napkins set in the dining room, rather than the breakfast room off the kitchen. The "good" dishes, the silver, the crystal — it all came out for Shabbos. But beyond that, familiar daily activities were suspended: there was no writing in my mother's house on Shabbos, and there was no riding, not on my bicycle and not in the car. (Unlike some people we knew, we did answer the phone — though nobody called — and turn on the lights.) The power of my parents' commitment had, as it was intended to, a lifelong effect on my sister and me.

The last decade has seen a renewal in appreciation of the joys of Shabbat. Many contemporary families view Shabbat as a chance for them to create a respite from the workaday world. They await Shabbat with happy anticipation of a family retreat at which they can share their delight in what they have as a family and as members of a larger Jewish community. It is an occasion, sometimes the only one during the week, for family conversation and bonding, for enjoying one another's company as well as the company of aunts, uncles, grandparents, cousins, and close friends. The centerpiece of this observance is Friday-night dinner. Countless people have told me that their families now regularly gather for Shabbat dinner. Though the teenagers and older children might scatter afterward, they do welcome the rituals, the conversation, and the spirituality of kiddush, candle lighting, and songs. Even unrelated people often celebrate in one another's homes for Shabbat dinner, an event that has become popular with many Jews who want to renew their faith and connection to their religion and four thousand years of Jewish history.

SABBATH HISTORY
AND OBSERVANCE

The Sabbath means, of course, more than simply a good meal; keeping it is a commandment. The fourth commandment is the only one among the ten that deals with a purely ritual observance — the Sabbath. Passages in Exodus, Ezekiel, and Isaiah reinforce the fact that Sabbath observance is absolutely central to Jewish life. Keeping the Sabbath is a sign of the covenant between God and Israel ("I gave them my Sabbaths, to be a sign between me and them, that they might know that I am the Lord that sanctify them," Ezekiel 20:12). The heart of this covenant is peacemaking and reconciliation; its goal is to create wholeness and peace — *shalom* in Hebrew — and harmony with friends, family, and colleagues. The Talmud says that if everyone observed two consecutive Sabbaths, the world would be whole and safe — redeemed.

The notion of formally establishing a day of rest was itself innovative, for no ancient society had such a concept, which was the precursor of the contemporary weekend. Though many ancients accused the Jews of laziness because of this suspension of work, Sabbath — which literally means "ceasing" — is in fact intended as a restorative, a time devoted to contemplation, study, recreation, and prayer. It is a weekly celebration of freedom from bondage, for it clearly emphasizes Jews' freedom from servitude to human masters. It stresses the freedom of the soul, of the intellect, and of the body — for servants, children, strangers, and even beasts of burden.

In his thoughtful and eloquent book *The Sabbath,* the late Abraham Joshua Heschel observed: "The meaning of the Sabbath is to celebrate time rather than space. Six days a week we live under the tyranny of things of space; on the Sabbath we try to become attuned to holiness in time. It is a day on which we are called upon to share in what is eternal in time, to turn from the results of creation to the mystery of creation; from the world of creation to the creation of the world."

Again and again, Heschel, who was professor of ethics and mysticism at the Jewish Theological Seminary, also reminds us what a gift God gave the Jews in the Sabbath, for, unlike Yom Kippur, it is dedicated to pleasure as well as to spiritual goals. To "call the Sabbath a delight" — Oneg Shabbat — (Isaiah 58:13) is to appreciate the potential joys of the day: things like beautiful clothes, delicious food, and marital relations. It is a day to be free from anxiety; it is, according to Heschel, "a day for praise, not a day for petitions." We don't make bargains with God on Shabbat but rather find joy in prayer and contemplation. On this day, activities such as fasting, mourning, demonstrations of grief, weddings, and funerals are forbidden. Shabbat takes precedence; it must be savored on its own, unadulterated, with an undistracted focus.

Attendance in synagogue has always been the most significant spiritual activity of Shabbat. At every time in the history of the Jewish people and in every place where they have dwelt, public worship and the keeping of the Sabbath, along with the observance of the rules of kashrut, have been the keystones of Jewish identity. Historically, attendance at synagogue has given the rabbis a forum to educate and inspire Jews through teaching and prayer. Shabbat rituals have been under their authority since the destruction of the Second Temple in 70 C.E. This authority was confirmed with the writing of the Babylonian Talmud in the sixth century, when the prestige of the Babylonian academies reached their height. During this and the earlier Talmudic period, Torah instruction centered on scriptural readings was codified and, inevitably, published for use by Jews everywhere.

Halakah, the overall term for Jewish law, rules all aspects of Jewish life, including Shabbat. It is based on biblical statutes and commandments in the written and oral Torah and on the interpretation of rabbinic scholars handed down through the ages in the Responsa and Commentaries. Halakah deals with ethical and religious obligations; it focuses on the fulfillment of the commandments; it applies the abstractions of the Torah to the deeds of everyday life.

Though Shabbat is joyous and serene, it is also a day of prohibitions, designed to stress its special nature. Sabbath laws prohibit those labors associated with the construction of the Tabernacle in the wilderness. These labors represent the archetype of creativity, and to appreciate and relish that creativity one must abstain from manual labor. The rabbis of the Talmud specified those activities that would disturb the spirit of the day and prevent people from knowing its holiness and joy. Specifically, the Torah demands: "Let no man go out of his place on the seventh day," Exodus 16:29; which the rabbis interpret as a prohibition against carrying anything; lighting a fire ("Ye shall kindle no fire throughout your habitations upon the Sabbath day," Exodus 35:2–3); and engaging in work (Exodus 20:10; Deuteronomy 5:14). This limited catalog of forbidden activities was expanded by the rabbis into seven categories, each refined and enumerated to total thirty-nine restrictions: growing and preparing food (no sowing, reaping, plowing, binding sheaves, threshing, winnowing, etc); making clothing (no bleaching, carding, spinning, weaving, making two loops, making two stitches, etc); leatherwork (no hunting a gazelle, scraping it or cutting it up, salting it or curing its skin, etc.); and writing (writing two letters of the alphabet, erasing in order to write two letters of the alphabet); providing shelter (building, demolishing); creating fire; completing work in progress; and transporting goods. In the third century, Rabbis Johanan and Simeon ben Lakish spent more than three years concentrating on what the Talmud referred to as the "forty minus one" classes of forbidden work, from which they compiled a list of thirty-nine specific acts covered by each category, for a total of 1,521. Later rabbis specified three additional prohibited categories: *muktzah:* items forbidden for use shouldn't even be handled (don't finger your knitting needles); *sh'vut:* if a task is forbidden to a Jew, a non-Jew shouldn't be asked to carry it out (the Shabbos goy was exempt from this restriction because he wasn't asked specifically to do the chore on the Sabbath); and *uvdin d-chol:* such weekday events as business discussions or office work or even sports are forbidden, though sports can be exempted by the creation of an *eruv,* which symbolically transforms a public space into a private one by creating an enclosure that allows Jews to carry equipment (as well as keys and other necessary personal items) and push baby strollers. The *eruv* is a legal fiction that makes the area it encloses halakicly private property and therefore not a violation of Exodus 16:29: "Let no man go out of his place on the seventh day."

Choosing or making Shabbat is a personal and family commitment to peace and prayer, a special day, separate and distinct from the other six. Its significance as a moral and spiritual restorative, an intellectual and theological oasis, cannot be overstated. It is the most powerful force in Judaism. For thousands of years it has lifted its followers out of the drudgery and toil of work; it has allowed every Jew, rich and poor, to experience leisure and the joys and dignity of the Torah. The weekly celebration has been the strongest tie of Jews to their religion. "More than Israel has kept the Sabbath, the Sabbath has kept Israel" was the keen observation of Ahad Ha'am (Asher Ginsberg), a Russian-born Hebrew writer and thinker who died in 1927 in Tel Aviv.

The entire week preceding Shabbat is, in a sense, preparation for it. Shabbat marks a weekly deadline for cleaning the house, polishing the silver, and getting the laundry done. A Shabbat aura is actually created by the look and feel of the home, because it is there, not the synagogue, where the festive mood is established, where the respect for "the Queen" or "the Bride," as Shabbat is sometimes called, is palpable. A midrash portrays God as saying, "A precious jewel have I in my possession and Sabbath is its name." These images of radiance and beauty, majesty and grace, purity and royalty, convey the importance of the day and the respect, awe, and love in which observant Jews hold it.

To ensure a sense of celebration, three feasts are ordered for Shabbat: Friday dinner, Saturday lunch, and shalosh seudot (also called *shaleshudos, seudah shlishit*), which is a light meal served between mincha and maariv, the afternoon and evening synagogue services. Among Hasidim, a fourth meal extends the celebration. This melave malkah is the farewell to the Sabbath Queen; its literal meaning is "to escort the Queen." The four core rituals for Friday-night observance at home are candle lighting, blessings over wine, blessings over bread, and the eating of the meal. There are three religious duties that every Jewish woman must perform, and two of them relate to Shabbat: separating the challah (see page 20) and lighting the Sabbath candles. (The third is ritual purification in the *mikvah*.)

The Jewish calendar is a lunar one, with the new month beginning with the first sliver of a new moon. The first day of each month begins at night, as do all the days following. *Hadlakot nerot,* candle lighting, takes place eighteen to twenty-one minutes before sunset, because the candles must be lit before the actual arrival of Shabbat. The ritual of candle lighting probably originated as a way to provide light for a little longer into Shabbat without violating the prohibition against "lighting a fire." A minimum of two candles are lit, symbolizing the two forms of the fourth commandment: "remember" the Sabbath day to keep it holy (Exodus 20:8) and "observe" the Sabbath day to keep it holy (Deuteronomy 5:12). Many women light an additional candle for each child in the family. Normally, a blessing is recited before the mitzvah of candle lighting. On Sabbath, however, the candles are lit first and the benediction recited afterward because the blessing ushers in the Sabbath, after which it is forbidden to light a flame. Jewish women encircle the light three times with their hands and repeat each time: *Baruch hu u'varuch shemo* ("Blessed be He and blessed be His name"). They then cover their eyes with their hands while reciting the blessing *Baruch ata adonai elohainu melech ha'olam asher kidshanu b'mitzvotav v'tzivanu l'hadlik ner shel shabbat* (" Blessed art Thou, Lord our God, King of the universe who has sanctified us with His commandments and commanded us to kindle the Sabbath lights"). Just after the candle lighting, members of the household greet one another with the words "Shabbat Shalom."

The blessing over the wine is called the kiddush, a word derived from *kadosh,* which means "holy." It is a biblical requirement to sanctify the Sabbath with a verbal declaration ("Remember the Sabbath day to keep it holy," Exodus 20:8) at its beginning and a declaration of separation (havdalah) at its conclusion. The sages ruled that this sanctification should be conducted over a glass of wine, the universal and ancient symbol of festivity. Though any glass can be used, a decorative ritual kiddush cup is appropriate to the mitzvah. The cup is raised and the head of the household recites a passage from the Torah that recounts the creation of the world; a second blessing is recited that recalls three Shabbat themes: the Creation, the Exodus, and the sanctity of the Sabbath. Separating these passages is the traditional blessing over wine: *Baruch ata adonai elohainu melech ha'olam borai pri hagafen* ("Blessed art Thou, Lord our God, King of the universe who creates the fruit of the vine").

In traditional households, symbolic hand washing follows the prayer over wine, and it is immediately followed by the blessing over the challahs. The cloth covering the breads is removed, and the head of the household recites: *Baruch ata adonai elohainu melech ha'olam ha'motzi lehem min ha'aretz* ("Blessed art Thou, Lord our God, King of the universe who brings forth bread from the earth"). The bread is then cut and distributed around the table.

Other rituals include *tzedakah,* the giving of charity. It is a mitzvah to put aside money for charity before candle lighting (it's forbidden to handle money on the Sabbath). Although metal cans called *pushkes* in Yiddish typically represent various Jewish charities, any can or jar will do. Hospitality is another mitzvah associated with Shabbat, a day when no one should be without a celebratory meal. As for a seder, travelers and people without families should be invited to share Shabbat.

Many families greet the Sabbath with songs. Two closely associated with the day are "Shalom Aleichem," an invocation of angels thought to hover close on Shabbat; and "Shabbat Shalom," whose lyrics are those two words only. Blessings are recited for children (for boys: "May God make you as He did Ephraim and Menasheh"; for girls: "May God make you as He did Sarah, Rebecca, Rachel, and Leah"); husbands recite to their wives the words of Ayseht Chayil (Woman of Valor) from Proverbs 31: "A good wife who can find? She is worth far more than rubies." Her virtues are enumerated: generosity, industry, business acumen, beauty, cheerfulness, loving-kindness, wisdom. The meal ends with grace, *birkat hamazon* (blessings for food), which begins with Psalm 126. A series of blessings and prayers set to a sequence of melodies thanking and praising God follows.

Saturday morning is spent in synagogue: the weekly portion of the Torah is read as part of the elaborate morning service. There is usually a kiddush for the congregation. The meal served after the morning service is the most challenging of the Shabbat meals, as it is normally served hot while observing the prohibition against lighting fire. Dishes like cholent, dafina, and adafina (see page 153) — variations on the slow-cooked meal — are the clever response by the Jewish housewives to the prohibition.

The afternoon is often given over to Torah study, family discussions, strolling, reading. The third meal is eaten in the very late afternoon, between the mincha and maariv services, before sundown. Usually simple, this seudah shlishit (literally, "third meal"), is often just challah and herring.

The Sabbath ends at nightfall, which is determined not by when the sun sets but by when three stars are visible. Just as Shabbat is welcomed with a kiddush, it ends with havdalah, which means division or separation. This ceremony of escorting the Sabbath out, and separating it from the coming week, is said over a cup of wine, with two additional blessings made for fragrant spices *(besamim)* and light *(ner)*. It is most often concluded at home, after evening services. The tradition of sweet spices may have begun with the burning of spices and herbs as part of any special meal. A folk explanation has it that an extra soul *(neshama yeterah)* descends from Heaven for Shabbat, and when it leaves, the body is faint and needs reviving; the spices renew some of the lost spiritual strength. The spices also provide strength for the coming week. The light, *ner,* is the first act of the new week and recalls the first act of creation, which marked the first day of the week, when God said "Let there be light." It is also considered proper that the first light struck after Shabbat have religious purpose. Both the box that holds the spices and the havdalah candle are decorative. The candle is made of two or more braided wicks, since a strong flame is required. The spice boxes are beautiful objects, often made of silver or wood.

The havdalah service begins with verses culled from Isaiah, Psalms, and the Book of Esther, and concludes with a fourth blessing over divine acts of separation: "Blessed art Thou, Lord our God, King of the universe who makes a division between the sacred and the secular, between light and darkness, between Israel and the other nations, between the seventh day and the six days of creation. . . ."

SHABBAT FOOD/JEWISH FOOD

Traditionally, the best food is reserved for Shabbat; the first seasonal fruits and vegetables are served on Friday night. The Mishnah stipulates serving two main courses — both meat and fish — on Sabbath. This and the mention of hamin (see Cholent, page 153) for Shabbat and lamb for Pesach are the only specific holiday foods mentioned in the Bible or the Mishnah. In eastern Europe, supplying the family with meat *and* fish was an enormous burden to the impoverished Jews, and Yiddish literature is filled with stories of Jewish men struggling to provide a proper Shabbat dinner. The Sephardim, who lived in agriculturally rich areas, were, in general, less impoverished.

In North America, Shabbat cooking traditions have been established by the Ashkenazim — it was these eastern European Jews who gave force and identity to the hyphenate of culture and cooking known as Jewish-American food. Nearly two million Jews arrived in America between 1881, when revolutionary terrorists assassinated Czar Alexander II, and the start of World War I, thirty-three years later. Most of them were from eastern Europe — Russia, Poland, Lithuania, and Galicia. They left to escape pogroms, organized official anti-Semitism, crushing poverty, political tyranny, and conscription into the czar's army (with a term of service that often lasted for as long as twenty-five years). These Ashkenazim came to far outnumber the Sephardim — Jews who had been expelled from Spain in 1492 and who had been in America since the seventeenth century — and the German Jews who immigrated in force in the mid–nineteenth century and who were already highly assimilated into American life.

Like all immigrant cooks, the Jewish housewife brought only her "best" recipes to the New World. All the foods that are recognizably "Jewish" were served on the Sabbath and holidays. It wasn't until these women bought so-called Jewish cookbooks that they were taught assimilation. Mrs. Esther Levy's *Jewish Cookery Book,* published in 1871 in Philadelphia, offered kosher recipes, but *Aunt Babette's Cook Book* (1889) is filled with shrimp, ham, and oysters, as well as traditional German-Jewish holiday dishes. *The Settlement Cookbook,* published in 1901, was the most powerful force in the dilution of traditional Jewish food and influenced generations of Jewish cooks. Published by the Settlement House of Milwaukee, it was designed to make the immigrant Jewish housewife more comfortable in her new Midwestern environment. Recipes were sanitized: traditional chicken fricassee (see page 108), for example, turned into a Midwestern dish with baking powder biscuits!

"Best" dishes, no matter what their origin, continue to form the basis of Shabbat menus. But as Jews have historically adapted the laws of kashrut to locally available food, our conception of "best dishes" has expanded. As the descendants of eastern European Jews travel more around the world and certainly to Israel, from which they learn about Middle Eastern food, as more varied Jewish populations immigrate to America and Israel and invigorate their cuisines, as Jews assimilate into American culture, and as more foods are certified kosher (forty-one thousand as of 1998), the Shabbat repertoire expands.

The prohibition against lighting a fire still exists, so the observant Jew must finish dinner preparation and Saturday-lunch preparations before sundown on Friday. Flame-tamers or *blechs* are easy to come by; ovens with low settings and timers are a boon to the Shabbat cook. A cholent can easily be cooked at home as we no longer have to depend on the ovens of the village baker.

The question "What is Jewish food?" is difficult to answer. If it meant those foods eaten by Jews, the definition would be easy and would also include many prohibited foods and combinations. But as has been true throughout Jewish history, Jews in America adapt the rules of kashrut to the available food and the myriad culinary opportunities we find in this country. It is much easier to follow the laws of kashrut nowadays than it was even a generation ago. How common, therefore, is Rabbi Joshua J.

Hammerman's experience? In *The New York Times Magazine* he wrote, "More than anything else, the Jewish contribution to American culture has been the communication of the experience of marginality, or having survived Otherness. Oreo denial [until Nabisco replaced the lard with vegetable oil, these cookies weren't kosher] was for me a direct extension of Egyptian slavery — it made me uncomfortable enough to feel different and different enough to feel proud."

Jewish food, finally, is the symbol of celebration and penitence, of feasting and fasting, and is inextricably entwined in the fabric of Jewish life. The way Jews consume food, the way the meat is slaughtered and prepared, the laws and prohibitions relating to food preparation, the community with which these values are shared, all strongly relate to Jewish observance. Judaism is an evolving way of life, not just a system of dogma and doctrine. New traditions can be established, new foods introduced within the parameters of the Bible, the rabbis, and the ancient laws, without throwing out our grandmothers' kugels.

A NOTE ON THE RECIPES

While working on this book, I asked every Jew I knew or met: "What did you eat for Friday dinner when you were growing up?" To a person the answer was "Chicken, sometimes brisket." Nowadays, Shabbat observers, whether kosher-keepers or not, want more choices, and in this book I have tried to provide a range of recipes suitable for Shabbat. My standard for including a recipe was "Is it special?" Within the laws of kashrut, there are many, many foods available for the Sabbath cook that we don't necessarily think of as Jewish. Practically speaking, "Jewish" is really what's available locally that isn't *trayf.* There isn't anything particularly Jewish about spinach, for example, but it's widely available and it's good, and that makes it suitable for Friday dinner. In America, we don't have to eat cabbage and root vegetables exclusively; we needn't eat the ossified shtetl food of our ancestors in the name of "tradition." We should establish our own traditions. In *Shabbat Shalom* I've included many poultry recipes because they are traditional in every Jewish culture. From my friend who grew up in Baghdad ("Chicken pilau, every Friday," he told me), to my friends who grew up with me in New York, to Jews in India and Italy, chicken was often the centerpiece of the Friday-night meal. In America it was frequently accompanied by chicken soup; gefilte fish (if we were lucky); kugel, maybe; a green vegetable; and compote and mandlebrot. I offer many choices beyond roast chicken (though, naturally, I've included it), to expand the repertoire of Shabbat dishes. As our horizons have broadened, so should our food. Whatever the family considers special — and one woman I met makes lasagna for her family because they love it — should be considered suitable for Shabbat.

The recipes gathered here come from a variety of sources: traditional dishes that I grew up with, favorites of family and friends, experiments, and adaptations from books. During my many years as a cookbook editor, I've often translated recipes into kosher form as a kind of mental exercise; many of those are here, too.

All the food in *Shabbat Shalom* is kosher if you use kosher meats and fish and observe the laws of kashrut. Though margarine, nondairy creamer, and other substitutions are available, I have chosen to cook with olive or vegetable oil and drink my coffee and tea black. Margarine, it turns out, is not all that healthful; so why not use olive oil or even chicken fat? Most of the desserts are pareve (neither meat nor dairy), though some contain dairy products and are therefore forbidden after a meat meal. The increasing number of vegetarians will find enough grains and vegetables for a celebratory meal, and I've included a few nonmeat cholents as well.

We're lucky to live in a land of such plenty, to have available asparagus and tomatoes, rice and orzo, and inexpensive, already-koshered chickens and geese, foods and service unknown to my Russian great-grandmother. I urge you to establish your own "best" dishes, your own "special" Shabbat meals, and follow the lead of generations of Jewish cooks by adapting what's locally available to the laws of kashrut if you're a kosher-keeper. Create the warmth and joy of the Sabbath in your own home and enjoy a Shabbat Shalom.

CHALLAH

*See that the Lord hath given you the Sab-
bath; therefore He giveth you on the sixth
day the bread for two days.*

EXODUS 16:29

*And the Lord spoke unto Moses, saying:
Speak unto the children of Israel and say
unto them: When you come into the land
whither I bring you, then it shall be, that,
when ye eat of the bread of the land, ye shall
set apart a cake for a gift.... Of the first of
your dough ye shall give unto the Lord a portion of a gift throughout your generations.*

NUMBERS 15:17–21

THE BIBLE (NUMBERS 15:17–21) REFERS TO TWO TYPES of challah: the portion that was separated and given to the priests, and the twelve flat unleavened loaves, symbolizing the twelve tribes of Israel, that were placed every week in the Temple. Fresh loaves were exchanged every Friday for those baked the previous week. One of the miracles associated with challah is that the week-old loaves remained fresh. After the destruction of the First Temple, the home table replaced the altar and the twelve breads were replaced by Shabbat loaves. (Some people think that the traditional six braids symbolize the two rows of six loaves of this Temple's Shaw Bread.) The separation of a piece of dough "the size of an olive," also called challah, from the main dough is the interpretation of the quote above from Numbers. It is one of the three mitzvoth specifically given to women. (The other two are Shabbat and holiday candle lighting and regular purification in the *mikvah*.) Though this portion is no longer given to the *kohanim,* the mitzvah is still observed. The act proclaims the woman's belief in God as the provider of all things. A special prayer is said just before separating the dough. The separated challah is usually burned in the oven, preferably under the broiler. And it is burned because we are forbidden to benefit personally from it.

Jews bake two loaves of challah, to represent the double portion of manna God provided on Friday for Shabbat during their years in the desert. When the manna fell to the ground it remained fresh, protected by the dew, which is symbolized by placing a board beneath the bread and a beautiful, often embroidered, cloth over the bread. Many people sprinkle the loaves with sesame or poppy seeds, to symbolize the dew. Some people think that the two challahs, like the two candles lit on Shabbat, symbolize the two forms of the fourth commandment: "*Remember* the Sabbath" and "*Observe* the Sabbath day to keep it holy." It is another theory that the cloth is used to cover the challahs so they are not shamed by being blessed *after* the wine.

Since the Middle Ages, the elaborate shaping of challah has taken on symbolic and mystical meaning. In biblical times, challah likely resembled pita bread — flat and round. The braided loaves we now know as challah probably originated in medieval Germany, where it was called *berches* or *barches*. There are braids for Shabbat, probably because it makes a decorative loaf; a crown for Rosh Hashanah, the ring symbolizing the hope for a complete and harmonious year; a bird, traced to eighteenth-century Ukraine, for the pre–Yom Kippur meal: "May our sins be carried away by the bird." For the seventh day of Sukkoth, the loaf is sometimes marked with a hand, symbolic of reaching for blessings, or key shaped, that the door of heaven may be opened to admit prayers. The Purim loaf is long and braided, representing the long ropes used to tie Haman. You can experiment with shapes and braids — one, three, six — as well as the different recipes: savory or sweet, plain or fancy.

FAMILY CHALLAH

2 packages active dry or fast-rising yeast

¼ cup sugar

1 cup warm (about 105 degrees) water

2 large eggs

1 egg yolk

1 tablespoon salt

¼ cup vegetable oil

4 to 5 cups bread or all-purpose flour (see Note)

Oil for the baking sheet or loaf pan

Egg Wash: 1 egg plus 1 yolk beaten with 1 tablespoon water

Poppy seeds or sesame seeds for topping

1. In a large bowl, sprinkle the yeast and a pinch of the sugar over the water. Stir to dissolve the yeast. Add the eggs, egg yolk, remaining sugar, salt, and vegetable oil. Stir in 4 cups of flour.

2. Turn the dough out onto a floured surface and knead for 10 to 15 minutes, until the dough is elastic and soft, adding ¼ cup more flour at a time if the dough feels too sticky.

3. Transfer the dough to a lightly oiled bowl, turning it to coat all the surfaces with the oil. Cover the dough with plastic and set it aside until it is at least doubled in volume. It could take anywhere from 1 hour to 2 or 2½ hours, depending on the weather and the type of yeast you use.

4. Turn the dough out onto a work surface and knead it for just a couple of minutes. Return it to the wiped-out bowl, cover, and let rise again, until doubled in volume. An indentation made in the dough should not pop back.

5. Punch the dough to deflate it. Cut it in half. With your palms, roll each half into 2 long ropes, then cut each rope into 3 equal pieces. Roll the pieces into cylinders, elongating each cylinder with your hands, pushing from the center to the edges, tapering the edges. Each strand should be about 12 inches, with tapered ends. Place 3 ropes side by side. Beginning in the middle of the rope, pass the left-hand piece over the middle rope, then bring the right-hand piece over. Continue left over right, right over left, until you reach halfway. Pinch the ends together. Turn the rope so the bottom is now the top and complete the braid, this time going under each strand; pinch again. Repeat the process with the other 3 ropes.

6. Preheat the oven to 350 degrees. Lightly oil a cookie sheet.

7. Transfer the challahs to the cookie sheet. Brush them with some of the egg wash. Move the challahs to a warm place and let them rise again. Brush them again with egg wash and sprinkle them with poppy seeds or sesame seeds.

8. Bake the challahs in the preheated oven for about 35 minutes, until the bread is a deep rich brown and the bottom sounds hollow when tapped with your fingertips.

The bread will have a softer texture if you use bread flour, but it's good made with all-purpose flour, too.

To make the dough in a food processor: Sprinkle the yeast over ¼ cup warm water in the work bowl; pulse to dissolve. Because the motor becomes so hot, add ¾ cup ice water with the remaining ingredients and 2 cups flour; pulse and add more flour 1 cup at a time. Pulse until the dough forms a mass. Knead by hand for 10 to 15 minutes.

To make the dough in a standing electric mixer with a dough hook: Dissolve the yeast in the water in a small bowl with some of the sugar. Sift the flour into the work bowl, make a well in the center, and add the yeast and remaining ingredients. Mix at the lowest speed to prevent splattering, scraping the bowl and hook until the dough begins to cling to the hook, about 7 minutes. Knead at medium-low speed for about 5 more minutes, until the dough is smooth and almost cleans the sides of the bowl.

ON SHAPING CHALLAH:
For Shabbat, a braided loaf is customary. The three-rope free-form challah described above is the easiest to make. You can also roll the ropes thinner and make a four-strand or six-strand challah. The technique is the same, just slightly more complicated.

To make challah in a loaf pan, which will yield a regular rectangular loaf with a braided pattern on top, roll the ropes about 10 inches long; braid as above and slip the loaves into 2 oiled 9-inch loaf pans.

VARIATION:
For a slightly sweeter challah, add ½ cup honey in step 1. You can also add ½ cup raisins, for a festive loaf.

Challah

SWEET CHALLAH

2 packages dry yeast

2½ cups warm water (105 degrees)

7 to 9½ cups sifted unbleached flour

½ teaspoon cinnamon

1 tablespoon salt

1 teaspoon vanilla extract

4 large eggs

¾ cup corn oil

½ cup sugar

1 tablespoon poppy seeds or sesame seeds

1. Sprinkle the yeast over 1 cup of the warm water. Stir.

2. Place 3 cups of the flour in a large mixing bowl. Make a well in the center and add the yeast mixture. With a fork, gradually incorporate ½ cup of the remaining flour into the yeast. This done, stop stirring. Set the bowl in a warm place and let the dough sit for 45 to 50 minutes.

3. Sprinkle the cinnamon and salt over the dough. Add the vanilla, 3 of the eggs, the oil, and the sugar. Add the remaining 1½ cups of water and blend with the fork and then your hands. Add 2 cups of the flour, kneading. If the mixture is still too sticky, add up to 1 more cup of flour.

4. With a wooden spoon, keep stirring until you have a stiff dough. Knead for about 10 minutes; when the dough no longer sticks to your hands, it's ready. Shape it into a ball and cover. Let it stand for 20 minutes. Turn the dough out onto a floured board and knead it again for about 10 minutes. Turn it into a floured bowl, cover, and let it stand for about 30 minutes.

5. Turn the dough out again onto a board and knead it for just a couple of minutes. With a sharp knife, cut the dough into 8 equal pieces. Knead each small section briefly and shape it into a ball. Place each ball into a bowl to rest until all 8 pieces are shaped.

6. With your hands, roll 1 piece of dough at a time into a rope about 12 to 15 inches long.

7. For each loaf, align 4 ropes in front of you, side by side. Gather the tops together and pinch to seal. Braid by bringing the extreme left rope over the three ropes to its right to the center; do the same with the extreme right rope. Keep going until you have a pudgy loaf, stretching the ropes at the end to make them fit. Pinch together the bottom ends of the ropes. Separate the challah (see page 18) by pinching off a piece; and discard.

8. Oil a baking sheet. Carefully transfer the loaves to the baking sheet. Cover with a towel and let stand about 1 hour.

9. Preheat the oven to 325 degrees.

10. Beat the remaining egg with a pinch of sugar and brush the mixture all over the loaves. Sprinkle the loaves with poppy seeds or sesame seeds. Bake for about 1 hour.

APPETIZERS

*A wise word
is not a substitute
for a piece of herring.*

SHOLOM ALEICHEM

SOME OF THE RECIPES
in this chapter are good with a glass of
schnapps, after shul and before dinner.
Some are appropriate first courses, to be
eaten at table at the start of the meal. For
other first courses see Fish (page 63),
Vegetables (page 185), and Salads (page
213).

HERRING SALAD

This is a popular Ashkenazic appetizer — good on Friday night and good, too, anytime Saturday. The symbolism of the ingredients makes it an appropriate dish for Shabbat: the fish symbolizes fertility and the eggs are symbolic of the life cycle. Apart from that, it's a delicious appetizer, particularly satisfying with a glass of schnapps after shul.

1. Remove the crusts from the bread and soak it in the vinegar for about 5 minutes. Gently squeeze out the liquid.

2. Rinse the herring and pat it dry on paper towels.

3. In a wooden bowl, with a mezzaluna, chop together the bread, herring, eggs, onion, sugar, and apple. Alternatively, you could put the mixture through a meat grinder or the grater attachment of a food processor. You want some texture in this dish, so don't puree it. Stir in the oil and taste for tartness; add more sugar if necessary. The dish might also need salt. Mound the salad in a serving bowl and refrigerate it for at least 2 hours, then sprinkle it with the chopped scallion or parsley and serve with crackers, black bread, or raw vegetables.

VARIATION:

You can add 1 cup of sour cream or yogurt or ½ cup of each, 1 tablespoon of horseradish, and the juice of an orange to this salad.

2 slices white bread

¼ cup white vinegar

1 pound pickled herring fillets, fresh or bottled

2 hard-boiled eggs, quartered (see Note, page 38)

½ cup chopped onion

1 tablespoon sugar

1 tart apple, quartered, peeled, and cored

2 tablespoons vegetable oil

¼ cup chopped scallion or parsley, for garnish

BAKED HERRING

2 pounds potatoes

1 cup chopped onion

3 tablespoons shmaltz (page 36) or vegetable oil

½ cup bread crumbs

2 pounds pickled herring (see Note)

1 large apple, quartered, cored, and peeled

Herring was one of the few fish available to northern Europeans. The rabbis declared that salted fish was kosher even if it was prepared by non-Jews. They allowed it because it was not cooked and therefore was not "gentile cooking" *(bishuley acum)*. Herring is popular in Scandinavia, the Baltic states — Latvia, Lithuania, Estonia — and eastern Poland. Herring is a good source of protein, and Jews (and others) salted it, pickled it, and generally did what they could to preserve it through the winter. When they emigrated, Jews brought their taste for the fish with them. It's a good Shabbat appetizer and welcome, too, for shalosh seudot.

1. Boil the potatoes until just tender. Drain, peel, and slice them about ¼ inch thick.

2. Over low heat, sauté the onion in 2 tablespoons of the shmaltz or oil until they are very soft but not colored.

3. Preheat the oven to 375 degrees. With some of the remaining shmaltz or oil, grease an 8-inch gratin dish or other 6-cup baking dish. Sprinkle the dish with half of the bread crumbs.

4. Rinse the herring. Dice it, removing any bones you encounter.

5. Spread a layer of potatoes on the bottom of the gratin dish; cover with a layer of herring and a layer of onion. Finally, grate the apple quarters directly over the onion. Continue, finishing with a layer of potatoes. Sprinkle with the remaining bread crumbs and dot with the remaining shmaltz or oil, including any that remains in the onion pan. Bake the herring for about 30 minutes, until the top is lightly browned. Serve immediately.

NOTE:

Buy pickled herring fillets from an appetizing store or section of the supermarket. If you buy it bottled, discard the liquid and onions.

FISH COCKTAIL UNCLE LOUIE

My friend Gale Robinson grew up in a kosher home, and this play on Crab Louis was a Friday-night staple during her childhood. Crab Louis, according to *The Joy of Cooking,* was created by the chef at the Olympic Club in Seattle in the late nineteenth century. The Uncle Louie version, named for Aunt Helen's husband, Uncle Louis, was created in the 1950s on Long Island.

The components should be made hours in advance of serving; don't combine, however, until minutes before you serve.

1. Place the onion, bay leaf, and a few parsley sprigs with 2 cups of water or enough to cover the fish in a skillet. Bring the water to boiling, lower the heat to a simmer, and add the fish. Simmer until the fish is just cooked through, about 4 to 7 minutes, depending on the thickness of the fish. The fish should be white and firm. Remove the fish from the liquid and set it aside to cool. I put the fish in a small bowl that I then place in a larger bowl filled with ice water, but you can just let it cool on a platter. Discard the poaching liquid. Refrigerate the cooled fish.

2. Combine all the sauce ingredients and chill.

3. Just before serving, cut the fish into chunks, discarding the skin. As you handle the fish, feel for any bones and remove them.

4. Line a platter, individual plates, or stemmed glasses with lettuce. Place the fish on top and spoon the sauce over it. Sprinkle with parsley and serve, accompanied by the remaining sauce.

1 onion, peeled and quartered

1 bay leaf

Parsley sprigs

1½ pounds fillet of firm white fish: halibut, cod, scrod

Uncle Louie Sauce (see below)

Shredded lettuce or whole lettuce leaves

Chopped parsley

UNCLE LOUIE SAUCE

1 cup mayonnaise

¼ cup ketchup or chili sauce

2 tablespoons lemon juice

½ cup finely chopped scallion

1 tablespoon grated onion

A few dashes Tabasco

Appetizers

29

STUFFED GRAPE LEAVES

STUFFING

- 2 tablespoons olive oil
- 2 tablespoons pine nuts
- 1 cup chopped onion
- ½ cup uncooked white rice
- ¼ tablespoon sugar
- ½ teaspoon ground cinnamon
- Pinch ground cloves
- ⅛ teaspoon allspice
- 2 tablespoons currants
- 2 tablespoons chopped fresh mint
- 2 tablespoons chopped parsley
- Salt
- Freshly ground black pepper

- 1 1-pound bottle grape leaves
- ¼ cup olive oil
- 2 tablespoons lemon juice
- Lemon wedges
- Tomato wedges
- Chopped parsley

In Jewish communities along the Mediterranean, stuffed grape leaves were a common appetizer for Shabbat. This Turkish version is delicious. This is not quick to make, but it's not difficult. Grape leaves are sold bottled, preserved in brine. A one-pound jar holds about forty leaves.

1. To make the stuffing, heat the olive oil in a medium saucepan. Cook the pine nuts for 2 or 3 minutes, until golden; be careful, because they quickly turn from golden to burned. Add the onion, rice, sugar, spices, currants, and 1 cup of hot water. Stir, bring to boiling, cover the pan, and cook slowly for 15 minutes. The liquid should be absorbed and the rice tender. Set the filling aside to cool. Stir in the mint, parsley, salt, and pepper.

2. Bring 2 quarts of water to boiling. Gently remove the grape leaves from the bottle. Open them with care and quickly blanch them in the boiling water. Remove them carefully with a slotted spoon and drain them draped over a large bowl or colander (you'll probably need both). Cover your work area with a layer of paper towels. Working with one leaf at a time, gently open it, and shave off the stem with a sharp knife. Lay the leaf on a paper towel, vein side up, with the pointed end toward you. You can create layers of leaves, separated with paper towels. Shred the small and torn leaves and set them aside.

3. Preheat the oven to 350 degrees.

4. Place 1 tablespoon of the stuffing (more or less, depending on the size of the leaf) about ½ inch above the pointed end of the leaf closest to you. Bring the point up over the filling, fold in the sides, and roll. Roll the leaves neither so loose that the filling falls out nor so tight that the leaves are in danger of bursting.

5. As you finish each grape leaf, place it in a shallow casserole dish (roughly 13 × 9 inches), seam side down; if the dish won't accommodate all the leaves in one layer, you can create another layer. Scatter the shredded leaves over the stuffed ones. Pour 2 cups of hot water into the casserole dish; add the olive oil and lemon juice. Crumple damp parchment paper and place it over the grape leaves; weight it with one or two skillets or other pots small enough to fit inside the dish. Cook the stuffed grape leaves in the preheated oven for about 45 minutes. Check once or twice to make sure there's enough liquid in the pan, adding more water if necessary.

6. Cool the grape leaves; transfer them to a serving dish, cover, and refrigerate. Serve chilled, garnished with lemon and tomato wedges and chopped parsley.

AHEAD OF TIME NOTE:

The grape leaves will keep for several days, covered, in the refrigerator.

Yields about 1½ cups;
serves 6 as a first course

EGGPLANT SALAD

1 eggplant, 1 to 1½ pounds

3 garlic cloves, peeled and
coarsely chopped

½ teaspoon cayenne

2 teaspoons paprika

3 tablespoons olive oil

3 tablespoons lemon juice

1 tablespoon toasted cumin
seeds, ground (see Note,
page 123)

Salt

Freshly ground black
pepper

This is a good hors d'oeuvre, served as a dip with crackers, bread, or raw vegetables. It's a good first course, too, served on lettuce leaves, along with radishes and sliced cucumbers. It's also an excellent component of a vegetarian meal.

1. Preheat the oven to 450 degrees.

2. Pierce the eggplant with a knife or skewer it in several places to prevent it from exploding in your oven. Bake the eggplant on a baking sheet in the preheated oven for 1 hour, or until it is completely soft. Remove it from the oven, slice it in half the long way, and place it in a colander to cool and drain.

3. Peel the eggplant and place the flesh in a food processor with the remaining ingredients. Make a coarse puree. Let the puree stand at room temperature for an hour or so or cover and refrigerate. Serve at room temperature.

NAHIT

Chickpeas are traditionally served on the Friday night following the birth of a male child, in honor of his forthcoming bris. They are also served at Purim, as a reminder that Queen Esther ate a diet of grains and beans so as not to violate the laws of kashrut while she was living in the king's palace.

2 cups dried chickpeas
Salt
Freshly ground black pepper

1. Wash the chickpeas and pick them over. Soak them overnight in water to cover. Drain.

2. Place the chickpeas in a large pot (they will expand) and cover them with ample cold water. Bring the water to boiling, add salt, and simmer gently until the chickpeas are tender, anywhere from 1 to 3 hours, depending on the age of the chickpeas. From time to time, add enough boiling water to keep the chickpeas covered.

3. Drain the chickpeas. Return them to the pot to dry over medium-high heat, shaking the pan. Place the chickpeas in a serving bowl and sprinkle them with ample salt and pepper. Serve warm or at room temperature.

VEGETARIAN CHOPPED LIVER

1 pound green beans

2 tablespoons vegetable oil

2 cups minced onion

4 hard-boiled eggs (see Note, page 38), chopped

½ cup finely chopped walnuts

3 tablespoons mayonnaise

Salt

Freshly ground black pepper

There are a lot of versions of "mock" chopped liver and vegetarian chopped liver. This one is a classic — good for liver-phobes and vegetarians as well as carnivores and liver lovers. Serve as an appetizer, on lettuce leaves, or as an hors d'oeuvre, with crackers.

1. Top and tail the beans. Place them in a large quantity of boiling water. Salting the water just after you put the beans in will help keep their color. Cook the beans for 5 minutes, until they are tender. Plunge them into ice water and cool. Pat the beans dry and chop them finely — you will have about 2 heaping cups.

2. Heat the oil in a skillet and sauté the onion slowly, about 30 minutes. The onion should soften but not color.

3. In a mixing bowl, combine the beans, onion, eggs, walnuts, and mayonnaise. Mix well and taste for seasoning, adding salt and pepper. Transfer the mixture to a serving dish, cover, and refrigerate until ready to use, up to 24 hours.

NOTE:

If you want a more even and spreadable consistency, you can put the mixture through the shredding disk of a food processor.

CHOPPED LIVER

Chopped liver has been a staple of every Ashkenazic home since...since forever, as far as I can tell. Every cook has her own variation. This version is a recipe from my friend Gale Robinson. I first saw her ring-mold presentation when Gale returned to New York after ten years in Birmingham, Alabama, where everyone served chopped liver this way. Though I laughed at the pretentiousness the first few times I saw it, I came to expect it and, yes, actually like it. You can, of course, also pile this into a pretty bowl and serve it sprinkled with chopped parsley.

1. Preheat the broiler. Lightly grease a 2-cup ring mold.

2. Wash the livers under cold water and carefully trim them. Broil the livers until they are cooked but not dry and burned.

3. Sauté the onions slowly in 2 tablespoons shmaltz or vegetable oil until very soft but not brown, about 20 to 30 minutes.

4. Put the onions and the fat they were cooked in, the livers, and the peeled eggs through the coarse blade of a meat grinder. Alternatively, use the grater attachment (not the blade) of a food processor, putting the ingredients through the feed tube and processing until the texture is coarse — you don't want a puree.

5. Transfer the mixture to a bowl and add a lot of salt and pepper. Spoon the mixture into the prepared ring mold and cover it with plastic wrap. Refrigerate the chopped liver until hardened, about 3 hours or overnight.

6. Wash, dry, and stem the parsley.

7. When ready to serve, run a knife around the sides of the mold, including the center, and invert it onto a serving plate. Holding the ring mold and plate with both hands, give a downward shake. You should hear a *plop*. Lift off the ring mold, fill the center hole with parsley, and surround the ring with crackers, triangles of rye bread, or matzo during Passover.

1 pound chicken livers

2 medium onions, peeled and chopped

2 to 4 tablespoons shmaltz (page 36) or vegetable oil (shmaltz is better, much better)

3 eggs, hard-boiled and peeled (see page 38)

Salt

Freshly ground black pepper

Large bunch of parsley, washed, dried, and trimmed

Crackers, rye bread, or matzo for serving

SHMALTZ AND GRIBENES

6 ounces chicken fat

1 cup chopped onion

4 to 5 tablespoons shredded chicken skin

The thrifty Ashkenazic housewife used every part of the precious chicken, and the rendered fat from the chicken or a goose was the flavor most associated with the eastern European Jewish kitchen. The *gribenes* (cracklings) were a special treat, to be saved for kugels and other dishes, to which they added crunch and flavor. Often the butt of jokes, and a staple of Yiddish humor, the word *shmaltz* has come into English meaning "maudlin sentimentality." It's also used to mean good luck: as to have fallen into a tub of shmaltz.

One chicken won't yield enough fat, so save up. Keep a container or a plastic bag in the freezer with chicken fat taken from the necks of several chickens; when you have six ounces, it's time to render the fat.

1. Put all the ingredients in a large, heavy skillet. Cook over low heat for 30 to 45 minutes: the skin and onion should be lightly colored and floating in bubbling fat.

2. Strain the fat through a fine sieve. The gribenes are what's left in the strainer. Use them for Chopped Egg and Onion (page 38) or mashed potatoes, or in a kugel.

NOTE:

Fat from geese and ducks can be rendered in the same way.

MICROWAVE METHOD:

Phyllis Richman, a novelist and the distinguished restaurant critic of *The Washington Post,* suggested this method: Put fat, onion, and skin in a microwave-friendly container; lightly cover it with a paper towel. In 5 minutes, on high, you will have delicious chicken or duck fat; if you keep cooking for another 10 minutes or so, you will also have delicious gribenes.

EGGS

IN EVERY JEWISH COMMUNITY, Sephardic, Ashkenazic, and all others, raw egg is a symbol of fertility and the continuation of Jewish life; boiled or roasted eggs symbolize death and mourning and are served when mourners return from funerals. They are also eaten on Tisha B'Av, the ninth day of the Hebrew month of Av, which is the date commemorating the destruction of the Temple. Eggs are served at births and deaths, at the conclusion of Yom Kippur, at Passover, on Shabbat. Only eggs from kosher birds are allowed, and each cook is obliged to check for blood spots or other impurities, which would render the eggs unkosher. Eggs are considered pareve.

CHOPPED EGG AND ONION

6 hard-boiled eggs (see Note)

½ cup minced scallion, including some green tops

1 tablespoon gribenes (page 36)

Salt

Freshly ground black pepper

3 tablespoons shmaltz (page 36)

Lettuce leaves

2 tablespoons chopped parsley

Matzo, challah, or black bread, for serving

This is an evocative taste memory for many Jews. Our family ate it on Fridays, and on many other days, too. It is a custom to eat eggs on Shabbat, at Friday dinner or Saturday kiddush or shalosh seudot. Eggs and gribenes together in one recipe are an indulgence. It's good without the gribenes, just not as good.

1. Quarter the eggs and chop them, preferably in a wooden bowl with a mezzaluna.

2. Add the scallion and gribenes. Chop until the mixture is blended.

3. Add salt, pepper, and shmaltz. Chop just to combine. Taste for seasoning before serving on lettuce leaves, garnished with parsley and accompanied with matzo, challah, or black bread.

NOTE:

To hard-boil eggs, place raw eggs in a saucepan with cold water to cover. Bring to boiling, reduce the heat, and simmer for 12 minutes. Immediately put the eggs under cold running water. When cool, tap the eggs against a hard surface to crackle the shell all over. If the eggs must wait for a few hours, leave them in their cracked shells in cold water. Once shelled, you should use the eggs immediately.

AHEAD OF TIME NOTE:

You can make this up to 8 hours in advance of serving. Place the mixture in a bowl, cover, and refrigerate until ready to serve. Don't garnish until serving time.

DEVILED EGGS

I tend to forget about deviled eggs until someone serves them and I remember how delicious they are. Now that eggs have been rehabilitated, serve these as an appetizer, one half per serving, on lettuce-lined plates.

1. Slice the eggs vertically and carefully scoop the yolks into a mixing bowl. Mash them with a fork.

2. Combine the yolks with the mayonnaise, mustard, and cayenne. If you want a very smooth mixture, press the filling through a fine sieve. Add the parsley.

3. Using a pastry bag, decoratively pipe the yolk mixture into the whites. You can also pile the filling into the whites with a teaspoon. Refrigerate until ready to use.

AHEAD OF TIME NOTE:
These are best served the day they are made.

4 hard-boiled eggs (see Note opposite)

¼ cup mayonnaise

1 tablespoon Dijon mustard

Pinch cayenne

2 tablespoons finely minced parsley

HUEVOS
HAMINADOS

Long-cooked eggs are a Sephardic staple: they are eaten on the Sabbath as part of a postsynagogue brunch and as a first course for Friday-night dinner. Eggs are frequently added to hamin, the Sephardic Sabbath stew, which is roughly equivalent to the Ashkenazic cholent and the North African dafina.

Huevos haminados are braised with used coffee grounds and a lot of onion skins. Slow-cooked in a 200-degree oven or in a crock pot, the eggs take on a warm brown color. Their texture is lovely: a creamy yolk and firm white. The onion skins keep the eggs from cracking and impart a slight flavor; the coffee grounds also add color. Eggs that aren't eaten whole can be saved and served throughout the week in salads and garnishes.

Remove the loose skins from your onion basket and line a pan with an ovenproof handle with them. Add as many eggs as you'll need, a tablespoon or two of that morning's used coffee grounds, and a tablespoon or two of wine vinegar; cover with cold water. Bring to a simmer on top of the stove; cover the pot and place it in a preheated 200-degree oven. Cook for 6 to 12 hours.

SORREL-STUFFED HARD-BOILED EGGS

These eggs have been part of my cooking repertoire since I first saw Richard Olney's recipe in *Simple French Food* twenty years ago. I've taken some liberties with his recipe, but the conception is his. It's a lovely first course for Shabbat; serve each diner half an egg. You can adjust the recipe if you have more or fewer guests. For my taste, you can't have too much sorrel — just add it to the gratin dish.

4 hard-boiled eggs (see Note, page 38)

6 to 8 ounces sorrel, stems removed, washed, dried, and shredded

5 to 6 tablespoons olive oil

½ cup grated Parmesan cheese or bread crumbs

Salt

Freshly ground black pepper

1. Preheat the oven to 400 degrees.

2. Slice the eggs in half lengthwise. Remove the yolks to a small bowl. Add about one-third of the shredded sorrel and 2 tablespoons of the olive oil. Mash and combine with a fork. Add half the cheese or bread crumbs along with about 2 tablespoons of the olive oil and salt and pepper. The mixture should just hold together.

3. Toss the remaining sorrel with salt and pepper and 1 tablespoon of olive oil. Spread it evenly in a gratin dish into which the egg halves will fit snugly.

4. Fill the egg white halves with the sorrel and yolk mixture and place them on top of the sorrel in the gratin dish. Sprinkle the eggs with the remaining cheese or bread crumbs and drizzle with 1 tablespoon of the olive oil. Bake the eggs in the hot oven for 15 to 20 minutes. The bed of sorrel will be bubbling and the tops of the egg halves nicely colored.

SOUPS

If you refrain from trampling the Sabbath
And keep my holy day free from your
    own affairs,
If you call the Sabbath a Day of Joy [Oneg
    Shabbat] the Lord's holy day honored
And if you honor it by not plying your trade,
Nor seeking your own interest
Or attending to your own affairs
Then you shall find joy in the Lord,
And I will set you riding to the heights
    of the earth
And let you enjoy the heritage of your
    father Jacob —
For the mouth of the Lord has spoken.

ISAIAH 58:13–14

SOUPS MADE OF VEGETABLES AND pulses are the earliest known cooked foods. Earthenware cooking pots dating from the biblical era were used to make primitive soups. Vegetable soup is mentioned in a thirteenth-century document by Rabbi Meir of Rothenburg. In nineteenth-century Jerusalem, Sephardim drank soup nearly every day; in Lithuania, Jews made krupnik, a thick soup of barley, sometimes with dried mushrooms (see page 59), borscht from beets, and schav from sorrel. From earliest times, cooks knew soups' beneficial qualities and knew, too, how easy they are to prepare and how satisfying to eat.

We are blessed with a wide variety of beans, vegetables, meats, and poultry for soup making. And starting a meal with a nourishing soup offers wide textural and taste variety.

Some of the soups in this chapter are utterly traditional in one Jewish culture or another — chicken soup among the Ashkenazim, chickpea soup from Morocco, for example. Others are flavorful soups without cultural identification, but they're so good, they're good enough for Shabbat.

CHICKEN SOUP

No food is more deeply embedded in the Jewish psyche and associated with Jewish cooking than chicken soup, and few foods are so good and so good for you. It is a true restorative and starts many a Shabbat dinner in many a Jewish home. In my mother's home, it started *every* Shabbat dinner and that was just fine with us. The soup, *goldene yoich* (golden soup) in Yiddish, is a shtetl leftover — from one hen the thrifty cook could get soup, fricassee, cooking fat, and all the delicious boiled flesh to serve one way or another. Further, she was able to make good use of those hens who no longer laid eggs. This rich and delicious version uses two hens and requires not much work but a lot of time. I sometimes stretch it over two days — but there are shortcuts.

1. Remove the fat from the cavities of the hens and set aside for rendering (see page 36).

2. Place one hen in a stockpot with the water and half of the vegetables. The ingredients should barely be covered. Bring the water to boiling and immediately lower the heat. Skim the foam that rises to the surface and adjust the heat so that only a bubble or two appears on the surface of the liquid. Add the parsley sprigs and crushed peppercorns, partially cover the pot, and simmer for about 2 hours, skimming occasionally. The hen should be tender but not completely falling apart. If you have time, let the hen cool in the soup.

3. Place the hen on a board and remove the meat from the bones. Put the skin and bones back into the simmering soup (or bring to a simmer if the hen cooled in the soup). Cook for another hour or so. Reserve the meat for another use, such as Chicken Pie (page 100) or Middle Eastern Chicken (page 103).

(continued on next page)

2 6 to 8-pound stewing hens, including neck and giblets but not the liver

5 to 6 quarts water

4 large onions, peeled and halved

6 carrots, scraped and cut into large chunks

15 parsley sprigs

10 peppercorns, crushed

Parsley

Dill

Matzo Balls (page 47)

Mandlen (page 48)

Egg Kneidlach (page 49)

Potato Kneidlach (page 50)

4. Strain the soup into a large bowl and discard everything in the strainer. Cool the soup and refrigerate overnight. Remove the fat that has hardened on the surface.

   For a really superb soup, start again with the just-made defatted chicken stock, the second hen, the remaining vegetables, and just enough additional water to barely cover the ingredients.

5. Serve with chopped parsley or dill, and kneidlach or mandlen.

NOTE:

Chicken soup freezes very well. You can freeze it in ice-cube trays for easy removal of small amounts. Don't freeze all of it in one container, because it's unlikely you'll use all of it at one time.

I feel a little uneasy when there's no chicken soup in my freezer.

MATZO BALLS (KNEIDLACH)

Matzo balls (called *kneidlach* in Yiddish) are iconic: the quintessential Jewish food. There are only a few essential ingredients, though the kneidlach can be dressed up with some additional ones. These dumplings add substance to chicken soup, and with a few noodles in the soup along with some pieces of chicken, it's a meal in a bowl. For Shabbat, it's just the starter.

Most people strive for light matzo balls, not the "hockey pucks" or "bowling balls" that many cooks actually achieve. I think it's the rest in the refrigerator that results in light kneidlach; others think it's the use of seltzer in the batter. You decide.

4 eggs

½ cup water or seltzer

6 tablespoons melted shmaltz (page 36)

Salt

Freshly ground black pepper

1 cup matzo meal

1. Stir the eggs with a fork just to combine the whites and yolks.

2. Stir in the water or seltzer, the shmaltz, salt, and pepper. Gradually add the matzo meal, stirring all the while to eliminate lumps. Refrigerate the batter for at least 1 hour.

3. Bring a large pot of water to boiling.

3. With moistened hands, form the matzo balls using about 2 tablespoons of the batter for each ball. Drop the balls into the boiling water. When the water returns to boiling, reduce the heat so the water simmers, cover the pot, and cook for 30 minutes. Remove the balls with a slotted spoon, tasting one to make sure they're cooked through. Place one or two in the bottom of each soup bowl.

VARIATIONS:

Add 2 teaspoons of grated fresh ginger and a few gratings of nutmeg to the mixture before refrigerating. Add 3 tablespoons of minced parsley or 2 tablespoons of finely snipped dill to the mixture.

AHEAD OF TIME NOTE:

The kneidlach can be made a few hours in advance of serving. Place them on a platter and cover loosely with paper towels. The heat of the chicken soup will warm them.

Soups

SOUP MANDLEN

3 eggs

3 tablespoons vegetable oil

1 teaspoon salt

1½ to 2 cups all-purpose flour

Mandlen means "almonds," which is what these soup crackers resemble. They are simple to make and filling — assets to the poor shtetl Jews and a delicious legacy.

1. Preheat the oven to 350 degrees. Lightly oil a cookie sheet.

2. Combine the eggs with 1½ tablespoons of the oil. Add the salt and 1½ cups of the flour. Make a soft dough; if it's too sticky, add up to ½ cup more flour

3. Divide the dough into 8 to 10 pieces — small enough to make rolling the dough between the palms of your hands easy. Roll each piece into a rope about ½ inch thick. Cut each rope into ½-inch pieces and place on the cookie sheet.

4. Bake the mandlen for 20 to 30 minutes, shaking the pan occasionally so they color evenly. They are done when they are golden brown and firm. Cool them to room temperature before storing in an airtight container. To serve, place the mandlen in the bottom of the soup bowls before you ladle in the steaming hot soup.

EGG KNEIDLACH

These light dumplings are a nice alternative to matzo balls in chicken soup.

1. Bring a saucepan of water to simmering.

2. Break the egg into a medium-size bowl and beat lightly. Add the remaining ingredients, including the nutmeg if you wish, and mix to combine.

3. Keep a small bowl of cold water next to you. Form the dumplings with a long-handled ½-teaspoon measure, dipping the spoon into the cold water after each ball is formed. Tap the measuring spoon against the side of the saucepan to release the dumpling into the barely simmering water. Do this quickly and decisively. Cover the pan and cook for 25 to 30 minutes, until the kneidlach rise to the surface and are soft and light throughout (you'll have to taste one to make sure).

4. Remove the dumplings with a slotted spoon and drain them on a platter. To serve, place 2 dumplings in the bottom of each soup bowl; the steaming soup will heat the cool kneidlach.

AHEAD OF TIME NOTE:
You can make these dumplings early in the day you plan to serve them. Don't refrigerate them, but cover them loosely with paper towels.

1 egg
¼ teaspoons salt
⅓ cup flour
⅛ teaspoon baking powder
Pinch grated nutmeg (optional)

POTATO KNEIDLACH

1 pound potatoes

1½ tablespoons shmaltz (page 36) or vegetable oil

1 tablespoon flour or matzo meal

1 egg

1 tablespoon salt

Here's another delicious alternative to matzo balls. These dumplings are great in chicken soup and are a welcome addition to stews. They're good for Passover as well as Shabbat.

1. Boil the potatoes in a large quantity of water. Peel them and pass them through a food mill with the shmaltz or vegetable oil. If you mash the potatoes with an old-fashioned potato masher, the dumplings will have small lumps —"texture"; if you use a food mill, the dumplings will be smooth.

2. Bring more water to a simmer in the saucepan.

3. Add the flour or matzo meal, egg, and salt to the potatoes. Combine with a wooden spoon. Form the kneidlach with moistened hands, using a tablespoon measure for each. Drop them into simmering water and cook for 10 minutes. Remove the dumplings to a plate with a slotted spoon. To serve, place 3 or 4 dumplings in the bottom of each soup bowl. The heat of the steaming soup will bring the kneidlach to a good eating temperature.

AHEAD OF TIME NOTE:

You can make the kneidlach a few hours in advance. Leave them on the plate, covered loosely with paper towels.

ASPARAGUS SOUP

This soup is for spring, when asparagus is plentiful. It's delicious cold.

1. Remove the ends of the asparagus and cut the stalks into thirds. Reserve about a dozen tips to use as garnish. Boil the reserved asparagus for 2 minutes in the stock. Remove them with a slotted spoon and plunge them into ice water.

2. Heat the olive oil in a sauté pan and gently cook the shallot for 5 minutes or so. Add the flour and whisk until the mixture is smooth. Half a cup at a time to start, add the boiling stock, whisking to make it smooth. After 1½ cups are added, you can slowly pour in the remaining liquid, whisking. Add the asparagus pieces, cover the pan, and simmer for 30 minutes.

3. Puree the soup in a processor and taste for seasoning, adding salt and pepper if needed. Reheat before serving, garnished with the reserved asparagus tips and chives or scallion greens. Or cover and refrigerate for a minimum of 6 hours to serve cold.

NOTE:

The soup can be made a day or so in advance of serving. To store asparagus, leave the bunch tied and place it standing in an inch of water. Don't cover, but do refrigerate. The asparagus will keep for 4 or 5 days.

2½ to 3 pounds asparagus

2 cups chicken stock, diluted with 4 cups water (or use all water), boiling

3 tablespoons olive oil

4 tablespoons minced shallot

3 tablespoons flour

Salt

Freshly ground black pepper

Minced chives or scallion greens

CAULIFLOWER SOUP

2 large leeks, cleaned and sliced, including some pale green top

3 tablespoons olive oil

1 medium cauliflower (3 to 4 pounds), cut into small florets (about 6 cups, including tender stems)

1 pound potatoes, peeled and cut into large dice (2½ to 3 cups)

10 cups water

Salt

Freshly ground white pepper

¼ cup minced parsley

This is a white soup with just a touch of green. Given the "bride" metaphor, I think of white food as appropriate for Shabbat.

1. Sauté the leeks in the olive oil until very soft, about 10 minutes.

2. Add the cauliflower, potatoes, and water. Bring to a simmer and cook, partially covered, over low heat, for about 30 minutes, until the vegetables are very tender.

3. Puree the soup in a food mill or a food processor. You can also use an immersion blender, but I think the food mill is faster. The soup should retain some texture.

4. Reheat the soup, add salt and pepper to taste, and serve sprinkled with the parsley.

AHEAD OF TIME NOTE:
The soup can be made a day in advance; it can also be frozen.

CELERY ROOT AND BARLEY SOUP

This hearty winter soup is a wonderful start to a special meal. Its creamy white color is another appropriate welcome for "the Bride," as some refer to Shabbat.

Celery root or knob celery or celeriac is a delicious vegetable full of flavor. To cope with this gnarled root, slice off the leaves with a sharp knife. Peel the root with a vegetable peeler, using the knife for irregular knobs. Slice and dice with a large chef's knife.

¼ cup pearl barley
  Salt
2 cups sliced onion
2 tablespoons olive oil
1 large celery root, peeled and diced (about 5 cups)
5 cups chicken stock or vegetable broth
  Freshly ground black pepper

1. Stir the barley into 3 cups of water in a heavy saucepan. Add ½ teaspoon of salt. Bring the water to boiling, reduce the heat, and simmer for about 45 minutes, until the barley is tender. Drain, and discard any remaining liquid.

2. Sauté the onion in the olive oil over moderate heat. Add the celery root and sauté for 5 minutes. Add the stock, salt, and pepper. Bring the soup to boiling, reduce the heat, and simmer until the celery root is tender, 20 to 30 minutes.

3. Puree the soup in a blender or processor. Return the soup to the saucepan, add the barley, stir well, and heat.

AHEAD OF TIME NOTE:

The soup will thicken as it stands; thin with water or additional chicken stock.

FRESH TOMATO SOUP

8 pounds tomatoes

1 teaspoon salt

2 cups coarsely chopped onion

FOR EACH 1½-CUP SERVING:

1 teaspoon unsalted butter or olive oil

1 tablespoon finely chopped fresh herbs (parsley, basil, chives, alone or in combination)

2 tablespoons croutons (see Note)

In nineteenth-century eastern Europe, many Jews thought tomatoes contained blood and deemed them unkosher. They were also suspect because some thought them aphrodisiacs. In twentieth-century America, they are widely enjoyed by people of all religions.

My friend Arthur Schwartz, host of *Food Talk,* a daily radio show in New York, and author of several cookbooks, knows more about food than anyone I know. He is a wonderful cook and teacher. This recipe is from his book *Soup Suppers*.

Make this soup when you or your local greenmarket has an abundant tomato harvest. I always make a batch of this soup in September to keep in the freezer and eat until I can make more, ten or eleven months later.

1. Wash the tomatoes. Cut out the cores and cut the tomatoes into chunks directly into a 6-quart pot.

2. Add the salt and onion. Cover the pot and cook over medium heat. Simmer until the tomatoes are very soft, about 20 minutes or so, stirring from time to time.

3. Puree the tomatoes in a food mill; leave the seeds and skin in the mill. Stop when the puree becomes pale.

4. Reheat the soup to a simmer before serving it with the butter, herbs, and croutons. Or cool and chill the soup. Serve it cold with a dollop of sour cream or yogurt or the two combined, garnished with herbs and croutons.

NOTE:

To make croutons, trim the crusts from artisanal or packaged bread and cube the slices. Place the cubes on a cookie sheet in a preheated 350-degree oven. Bake them for 4 to 5 minutes, toss, then return them to the oven for another 5 minutes, tossing the cubes frequently. They should be brown, not burned. You can also fry the croutons in hot olive or vegetable oil, tossing constantly, then turn them out onto paper towels.

IRANIAN MEATBALL SOUP FOR SHABBAT

This recipe is adapted from *Faye Levy's International Jewish Cookbook*. In her introduction to the recipe, Ms. Levy tells us that this traditional Iranian dish, *gundi,* is popular with the large Iranian population in southern California. It's a hearty soup and can serve as a main course.

½ cup packed parsley leaves

1 cup canned chickpeas, rinsed and drained

1 onion, coarsely chopped

½ pound ground beef
Salt
Freshly ground black pepper

2 quarts chicken or goose stock (page 120)

1 pound potatoes, peeled and cut into large dice

2 cups diced carrot

1 tablespoon tomato paste

1 teaspoon toasted cumin seeds, ground (see Note, page 123)

¼ teaspoon turmeric

½ teaspoon red-pepper flakes

1 cup uncooked white rice

2 tablespoons chopped parsley

1. One at a time, without washing the bowl in between, and removing each as it's done to one mixing bowl, chop the parsley, chickpeas, and onion by pulsing in a food processor. Add the beef, salt, and black pepper to the bowl and combine.

2. Form the mixture into small meatballs, rolling tablespoonsful between the moistened palms of your hands; put the meatballs on a platter as each is done. You should have 25 to 30 meatballs. When all the meatballs are made, refrigerate them.

3. Bring the stock to a simmer and add the potatoes and carrot. Cook, covered, for 20 minutes. Add the tomato paste, cumin, turmeric, and red-pepper flakes. Carefully add the meatballs. Cover the pot and simmer for 30 minutes.

4. Cook the rice for 12 minutes in a large quantity of boiling water. Drain.

5. Spoon ¼ to ½ cup of rice into the bottoms of 8 to 10 soup bowls. Add the soup and meatballs, sprinkle each bowl with parsley, and serve.

AHEAD OF TIME NOTE:

The soup can be made up to 2 days before serving. Cool, cover, and refrigerate it after step 3, cooking the meatballs for only 15 minutes. Reheat the soup gently before serving. Don't cook the rice until you're ready to serve it.

LEEK AND POTATO SOUP

1 pound potatoes, peeled and quartered

3 or 4 medium leeks (1 pound), cleaned and thinly sliced, including tender green tops

Salt

2 quarts boiling water

Freshly ground black pepper

3 tablespoons butter or olive oil

This simple soup is inspired by a recipe of Richard Olney's, an American living in France who is one of the finest contemporary food writers and cooks. The soup is delicious with the addition of a pat of butter. If your meal is a meat one, add a few drizzles of olive oil instead.

Add the vegetables to the salted boiling water. Cook until the potatoes are tender, ½ hour or so. Pass the soup through a food mill. Reheat, taste for salt and add pepper, add the butter or olive oil, and serve.

LENTIL SOUP

Lentil soup may have been Esau's pottage: "And Jacob gave Esau bread and a pottage of lentils; and he did eat and drink, rose up and went his way. So Esau despised his birthright" (Genesis 25:34).

1. Pick over and rinse the lentils. Quarter one onion; halve and chop the others. Scrape and chop the carrot.

2. Place the lentils in a saucepan with 2 quarts of water, the quartered onion, carrot, celery, and garlic. Bring to boiling, reduce the heat, partially cover the pot, and simmer until the lentils are tender, 30 to 45 minutes, depending on their quality and age.

3. Heat the oil in a small skillet. Add the chopped onion. Fry until crisp and colored but not burned. Set aside.

4. Puree the lentil mixture in a blender, in a food processor, with an immersion blender, or through a food mill. Return it to the saucepan and stir in the cumin, salt, and pepper. Heat and taste for seasoning. Just before serving, stir in the lemon juice and garnish the soup with the fried onions.

NOTE:

As it stands, the soup will thicken. If it becomes too much of a "porridge" for your taste, thin it with a little water.

2 cups lentils, green or red

3 onions

1 carrot

1 large celery stalk, with leaves, chopped

2 garlic cloves, peeled and chopped

2 tablespoons olive oil

2 teaspoons toasted cumin seeds, ground (see Note, page 123)

1 tablespoon salt
Freshly ground black pepper

1 to 2 teaspoons lemon juice

MOROCCAN CHICKPEA SOUP

1 pound dried chickpeas

8 garlic cloves

1 large knucklebone

¼ teaspoon pulverized saffron

Salt

Freshly ground black pepper

¼ cup minced fresh coriander or Italian parsley

Chickpeas are among the earliest cultivated plants — they were grown in the Hanging Gardens of Babylon. The pale yellow legume grows two to a pod. They are featured in both Ashkenazic and Sephardic cooking. This soup is a traditional Friday-night dish in Morocco.

1. Pick over and wash the chickpeas.

2. Cook them in water to cover by at least 3 inches for 20 minutes. Let them cool in the cooking water.

3. While the chickpeas are cooking, peel and halve the garlic cloves.

4. When the chickpeas are cool, drain them in a colander and wash them under cold, running water.

5. Place the chickpeas in a Dutch oven with a tight-fitting lid. Add the garlic and knucklebone. Cover the chickpeas with 2 quarts of water, bring it to boiling, and for several minutes, skim the foam that rises. Add the saffron, salt, and pepper, reduce the heat, cover the pot, and cook for 1½ hours, or until the chickpeas are tender.

6. Remove and discard the bone. With a wooden spoon, mash the chickpeas; alternatively, put the soup through a food mill.

7. Reheat the soup over gentle heat, turn it into a tureen, garnish with coriander or parsley, and serve.

MUSHROOM-BARLEY SOUP

Another shtetl legacy, this hearty soup makes a fine meal, served with Russian Salad (page 228) and challah (page 20).

1. Place the mushrooms in boiling water to cover, remove from the heat, and soak for at least 1 hour.

2. In a large soup kettle over low heat, sauté the onion, leek, and carrot in the oil until soft but not brown, about 15 minutes.

3. Add the marrow bones, flanken, and 4 quarts of water. Bring to boiling, reduce the heat so the liquid just simmers, and skim the foam as it rises. After 20 minutes or so the foam will have subsided. Add the barley, bouquet garni, salt, and pepper. Partially cover the pot and simmer the soup for about 1 hour.

4. Strain the soaked dried mushrooms through a cheesecloth-lined sieve, reserving the liquid. Chop the mushrooms coarsely and add them along with 1 cup of their soaking liquid to the soup. At the same time, add the fresh mushrooms. Cook at a slow simmer for another hour or so, until the soup is thick and the meat utterly tender.

5. Remove the marrow bones and flanken from the soup. Skim off as much fat from the surface as you can. Discard the marrow bones and cut the meat off the flanken. Ladle the soup into large bowls, adding some meat to each. Garnish with parsley and serve.

½ cup dried mushrooms

2 cups chopped onion

1 cup chopped white of leeks (save the greens for the bouquet garni)

2½ to 3 cups grated carrot

5 tablespoons vegetable oil

1½ to 2 pounds marrow bones

3½ to 4 pounds beef flanken

¾ cup barley

Bouquet garni of inner leek greens (carefully washed), parsley sprigs, bay leaf, tied together in cheesecloth

Salt

Freshly ground black pepper

¾ pound fresh mushrooms, wiped clean and chopped (about 3 cups)

½ cup chopped parsley

NOTE:

If you have time, strain the soup and put the broth in the freezer or refrigerator until the fat hardens on the top and can easily be removed.

As the soup sits, it thickens. Add more water when you reheat it.

MUSHROOM SOUP

3 tablespoons olive oil

2 cups sliced onion

1 garlic clove, peeled and sliced

1 pound mushrooms, wiped dry and sliced (about 4 cups)

½ teaspoon dried rosemary

Nutmeg

Salt

Cayenne

Freshly ground black pepper

Mushrooms, fresh and dried, are a staple of eastern Europeans, Jews and non-Jews alike. This intense soup is delicious with a garnish of sliced raw mushrooms.

1. Heat the olive oil in a saucepan. Add the onion and cook slowly until it turns a rich brown, 30 minutes at least.

2. Add the garlic, mushrooms (reserving a few slices for garnish), rosemary, a grating or two of nutmeg, salt, a pinch of cayenne, and black pepper. Add 5 cups of water, bring to a simmer, and cook slowly for 30 minutes or so. Strain the soup and taste for seasoning. Return it to a simmer before serving, garnished with the reserved mushroom slices.

SPINACH SOUP

I love to start a meal with soup, and I often start meals with this one. It's good hot or cold, it can be made in advance, it's wonderful with frozen spinach, and it's very simple.

1. Cook the onion slowly in the olive oil for about 15 minutes. It should soften but not color.

2. Add the spinach and stir to combine with the onion. Add the chicken stock and bring to boiling. Add the rice, lower the heat, and season with salt, pepper, and a few gratings of nutmeg.

3. Cook the soup at a bare simmer, partially covered, for 15 to 20 minutes — until the rice is done.

4. Puree the soup with an immersion blender or in a food processor. Reheat, taste for seasoning, and serve. If serving cold, let the soup cool to room temperature before storing, covered, in the refrigerator, where it will keep for several days.

2 cups chopped onion

2 tablespoons olive oil

2 10-ounce packages frozen spinach, defrosted (see Note)

5 cups light chicken stock (see Note)

⅓ cup uncooked white rice

Salt

Freshly ground black pepper

Nutmeg

NOTE:

A quick way to defrost the spinach is to place it in a bowl of cold water when you start your preparations. Squeeze out the moisture before you proceed. If you don't have time even for that method, you can put the frozen spinach in with the cooked onion, cover the pan, and stir occasionally until the spinach separates and defrosts.

This soup is easily served as part of a vegetarian meal by substituting vegetable stock (or a cube) or water for the chicken stock.

SPLIT PEA SOUP

1 pound dried green split
  peas, well washed

2 pounds knucklebones

1 cup chopped onion

½ cup chopped celery

1 cup chopped carrot

1 bay leaf

  Salt

  Freshly ground black
  pepper

  Lemon juice

1½ pounds frankfurters,
  cooked (optional)

½ cup chopped parsley

This is a hearty start to a winter meal; with the addition of frankfurters, the soup can be the centerpiece of the meal.

1. Place the peas, bones, and 2½ quarts of water in a soup kettle. Bring it to boiling, skimming foam as it rises.

2. When the foam subsides, add the onion, celery, carrot, bay leaf, salt, and pepper. Lower the heat and simmer gently, partially covered, for 45 minutes to 1 hour; until the peas are tender, almost mushy.

3. Remove and discard the bones.

4. Puree the soup with an immersion blender or in a food mill. It will be thick. Taste — add lemon juice and additional salt and pepper if necessary.

5. To serve, cut in the frankfurters, if you are using them, and sprinkle each bowl with parsley.

AHEAD OF TIME NOTE:
The soup can be made in advance and reheated before serving.

FISH

*Shabbat without fish
is like a wedding
without dancing.*

YIDDISH PROVERB

IT IS CUSTOMARY FOR JEWS TO EAT
fish on Friday night. The blessing in Genesis: "Be fruitful and
multiply and fill the water in the sea," has served as a symbol of
fertility. Fish is also associated with the coming of the Messiah.
Mishnah writings on the Book of Genesis state that all creatures
were annihilated during the time of Noah and the Great Flood
except fish, because fish did not sin. As the celebration of the
Sabbath is considered preparation for the Messianic era, and
legend states that the Messiah will come in the form of a great
fish, Jews naturally include fish in their Sabbath meals.

To be considered kosher, fish must have scales and fins. Prohibited are shellfish, catfish, swordfish, monkfish, turbot, shark,
eel, ray, and skate. Sturgeon and their precious roe, caviar, are not
exactly kosher, but they are not exactly not kosher — ask your
rabbi if you want to know for sure. Traditionally, fish and meat
can be eaten at the same meal, the former preceding the latter, but
not on the same plate.

Many of the recipes in this chapter are good as first courses or
luncheon dishes. They can serve as main dishes, too, for those
non–meat eaters at your table.

BAKED CARP

Izaak Walton called the carp "the queen of the rivers: a stately, a good, and a very subtle fish. . . ." An ancient food of Asia, it was pond-cultured in China before Christ. It was introduced to Europe and then to America from Germany in the nineteenth century. A prolific breeder and bottom-feeder, its habits deny sun-dependent plants and plankton the sunlight they need to live, making the carp an invasive, unwelcome fish. Nonetheless, its flavor is delicious. Carp is an ingredient in gefilte fish (see page 75), and eastern European Jewish housewives stuffed carp slices. *Larousse Gastronomique* has four recipes for Carp à la juive (Carp Jewish-style), which is poached carp served cold in its own jelly. The Polish version is sweet, the Russian tart.

This baked carp is a recipe of my friend Johanna Hecht Sokolov. Her mother made it and we don't know the origin, but we sometimes have it on Passover.

4½–5 pounds carp with large bone in

1 head garlic

1 tablespoon kosher salt

¼–½ teaspoon paprika

1. Ask the fishmonger to cut the carp so the pieces look like spareribs. Each piece should have a center bone.

2. Preheat the oven to 375 degrees.

3. Separate the garlic cloves and remove the skin from each clove. Place the garlic in a mortar with the salt. Pound to a paste with a pestle. Stir in the paprika.

4. Spread the garlic mixture over the carp slices.

5. Spread the carp in one layer on a cookie sheet. Bake in the oven for about an hour, until the slices are nicely browned.

6. Let cool to room temperature before serving.

- 3 pounds all-purpose potatoes
- 3 tablespoons olive oil

  Salt

  Freshly ground black pepper
- 2 cups minced onion
- 2 cups chopped canned whole tomato
- 3 pounds bluefish fillets
- 3 tablespoons chopped parsley
- 1 tablespoon minced chives

ROASTED BLUEFISH AND POTATO CASSEROLE

Bluefish has an intense flavor and oily texture; many people consider it "fishy," but I regard that as a compliment to fish. Here the potatoes act as a foil for the fish and the acidity of the tomatoes contrasts well with the richness of the fish. Cook the bluefish the day you buy it. This recipe is an easy-to-prepare main course for a meatless meal; it's good, too, as a first course to a more elaborate meal.

1. Preheat the oven to 400 degrees.

2. Boil the potatoes until barely tender, about 15 minutes. Peel and slice them ¼ inch thick.

3. Use a little olive oil to grease the bottom of a 2- to 3-quart shallow baking dish (a 9 × 13–inch rectangle works well; the fish fillets should cook in one layer). Layer the potatoes in the dish, adding salt and pepper. Roast for a few minutes while you continue with the recipe.

4. Heat the remaining olive oil in a skillet and sauté the onion slowly, without allowing it to color. Add the tomato and cook for 5 minutes.

5. Cover the potatoes with the onion-tomato mixture; season with salt and pepper. Lay the fish fillets on top. Roast the casserole in the preheated oven for 15 minutes, until the fish is cooked through. Sprinkle it with parsley and chives before serving.

BRAISED COD WITH CHICKPEAS

This dish is a characteristic Moroccan Jewish preparation. North Africans, Jews and non-Jews alike, are particularly skilled at cooking fish because the long coastline yields so much. Dried chickpeas, a staple starch in the Mediterranean, traveled with the Jews when they emigrated.

1. If canned chickpeas are used, rinse and drain them. Combine the cooked or canned chickpeas in a saucepan with the garlic, peppers or flakes, 3 tablespoons of the olive oil, and ¼ cup of water. Bring the liquid to a simmer, cover the pot, and simmer for 20 minutes.

2. Preheat the oven to 400 degrees.

3. Remove and discard the whole peppers, if you used them. Add the cumin to the chickpeas and spread half the mixture in the bottom of a 9-inch-square baking dish. Place the fish on top, sprinkle with salt and pepper, and finish with the remaining chickpeas. Drizzle the remaining 3 tablespoons of olive oil over the top. Cover and bake in the preheated oven for 30 minutes, until the fish is just flaky but not falling apart; check after 20 minutes.

4. Serve the fish hot or warm, garnished with cilantro or parsley and lemon wedges.

NOTE:

For dried chickpeas, soak ½ pound (1¼ cups) overnight, drain, rinse, and cook in water to cover for 1 to 1½ hours, depending upon their age. If you don't have time for overnight soaking, cover the chickpeas with cold water, bring them to boiling, turn off the heat, cover the saucepan, and set them aside for an hour, then cook them as directed above.

3 cups cooked chickpeas (see Note), or 2 15-ounce cans

6 or 7 large garlic cloves, peeled and sliced

4 or 5 whole hot peppers or 1 teaspoon red-pepper flakes

6 tablespoons olive oil

½ teaspoon toasted cumin seeds, ground (see Note, page 123)

2 pounds cod fillets, about 1 inch thick

Salt

Freshly ground black pepper

Cilantro or parsley sprigs

Lemon wedges

CHOUCROUTE OF FRESH AND SMOKED SALMON

2 cups minced onion

2 tablespoons olive oil

1 pound fresh sauerkraut (see Note), drained

1 cup dry white wine

1 bay leaf

6 juniper berries or ¼ cup gin

1 teaspoon coriander seeds ground in a mortar with a pestle

SAUCE:

⅓ cup minced shallot

¾ cup dry white wine

3 tablespoons white-wine vinegar

Salt

Freshly ground black pepper

½ teaspoon fennel seeds, ground in a mortar with a pestle, or ¼ cup minced fresh dill

1 cup crème fraîche or heavy cream

½ pound (2 sticks) cold butter

2 pounds fresh salmon, cubed

⅓ pound smoked salmon, diced

1 pound egg noodles, cooked in time to serve with the choucroute

On page 143 there is a recipe for Choucroute Garni, the great Alsatian meat and sauerkraut dish. This recipe for Salmon Choucroute was sent to me by David Downie and Alison Harris, an American couple who live in Paris and have published a glorious book, *Enchanted Liguria*. Alison is a photographer and David a journalist and they know good food. Regrettably, they do not remember the provenance of the recipe. The translation from French is mine. Don't be put off by the cream and butter — the dish serves six, and it's Shabbat, after all. If that excuse doesn't work for you, this dish is delicious — excellent, really — without any sauce at all. The choucroute is also good cold — either as a leftover for Shabbat lunch or as an appetizer on Friday night. Cold, it's good with drained plain yogurt with a lot of dill cut in.

1. Preheat the oven to 350 degrees.

2. In an ovenproof casserole, sauté the onion slowly in the oil for 10 to 15 minutes. Add the sauerkraut, white wine, bay leaf, juniper berries or gin, and coriander. Add a cup of water. Cover the casserole and cook the sauerkraut in the preheated oven for 2 hours.

3. To make the sauce, put the shallot, white wine, wine vinegar, salt, pepper, and the ground fennel seeds in a saucepan. (If you use dill, don't add it to the sauce until just before serving.) Bring the liquid to boiling and reduce it by three-quarters, to ¼ cup; this will take about 8 minutes after the liquid begins to boil. Add the cream and reduce by half. Off the heat, beat in the butter; keep the sauce warm over a very low flame.

4. Place the cubes of fresh salmon in the casserole and toss so they are covered with sauerkraut. Return the dish to the oven for 8 to 10 minutes. Just before serving, sprinkle the choucroute with the smoked salmon. Serve with the sauce and boiled noodles.

AHEAD OF TIME NOTE:

You can make the sauerkraut up to a day in advance and reheat before continuing.

NOTE:

Fresh or new sauerkraut is available in bottles in the supermarket. The fully fermented sauerkraut is too strong for this dish.

COLD FRIED FISH

4 4-ounce fillets of firm-fleshed white fish (cod, scrod, halibut, sea bass, flounder)

Salt

½ cup peanut or vegetable oil

⅓ cup all-purpose flour

1 large egg, lightly beaten

⅓ cup fine bread crumbs or matzo meal

¼ cup minced parsley

Lemon wedges

Cold fried fish was brought to England, via the Netherlands, by the Marranos fleeing the Iberian Peninsula in the fifteenth and sixteenth centuries. Thomas Jefferson discovered and praised "fried fish in the Jewish manner." It was also praised by other gourmets, including both Hannah Glasse and Eliza Acton in the mid-eighteenth century. An eastern European Jewish fishmonger, Joseph Malin, is credited with combining this staple Jewish dish with the fried potatoes of a neighboring Irish shop, creating in 1845 the first fish-and-chips shop. Fried fish remained, without the potatoes, the most popular Jewish fish preparation in England and is often served as a first course for Friday-night dinner.

1. Sprinkle the fillets with salt and barely cover with water. Let soak for an hour in the refrigerator. Remove the fillets, rinse, and pat dry with paper towels.

2. Heat 1 inch of the oil to medium-hot in a large skillet.

3. Dip the fish first in flour, then in egg, then in bread crumbs or matzo meal. Keep the coating thin by waving the fillets gently after applying each coating.

4. Fry the fish in the heated oil in one layer. The temperature of the oil is a little tricky: you don't want to burn the exterior without cooking the inside. The oil should sizzle gently when the fillets are added.

5. Remove the fish to paper towels and serve warm or at room temperature, sprinkled with parsley and accompanied by lemon wedges.

VARIATION: MARINATED FRIED FISH
Bring to boiling 1 cup of cider vinegar, 1 teaspoon of sugar, 1 bay leaf, 3 peeled and sliced garlic cloves, and 5 crushed peppercorns. Simmer for 5 minutes. Let the vinegar cool for a moment and then pour it over the fried fish. Marinate the fish for 24 hours, turning occasionally. The dish will keep for a week, refrigerated.

FISH BALLS IN LEMON SAUCE

This piquant Moroccan first course is often served on Shabbat, perhaps because it has no bones. The fish is colored by the saffron and turmeric in the poaching liquid and is a beautiful orange-gold — very festive. It's a variation on Ashkenazic gefilte fish and very easy to make. It's good at room temperature or cold.

2 pinches saffron threads

½ teaspoon turmeric

3 tablespoons vegetable oil

3 tablespoons fresh lemon juice

1½ pounds skinless, boneless scrod, cod, flounder, or other white-fleshed fish

1 small onion, quartered

2 tablespoons parsley sprigs

2 strips lemon peel, removed with a vegetable peeler

Grated nutmeg

Salt

Freshly ground black pepper

½ cup bread crumbs

2 tablespoons drained capers

1 tablespoon Dijon mustard

1. Combine the saffron, turmeric, vegetable oil, and lemon juice with 3 cups of water in a Dutch oven or other wide pot. Bring the liquid to boiling, reduce the heat, and simmer while you prepare the fish.

2. Chop the fish into large pieces and place them in a food processor, fitted with the metal blade, along with the onion, parsley, lemon peel, and a few gratings of nutmeg. Process until you have a smooth mixture. Turn the fish mixture into a mixing bowl and add salt and pepper and the bread crumbs. Mix well.

3. With moistened hands, form the fish into balls about the size of golf balls. Add the fish balls to the simmering liquid and cook, uncovered, for 20 minutes. With a slotted spoon or flat skimmer, transfer the fish balls to a platter.

4. Add the capers and mustard to the poaching liquid and pour it over the fish balls. Let the fish balls stand at room temperature for an hour or so before serving, or cool and refrigerate.

FISH CAKES

1½ pounds cod, scrod, or
other white-fleshed fish,
or a combination

2 tablespoons minced
scallion or shallot

¼ cup minced parsley

1¼ cups fine bread crumbs or
matzo meal

2 eggs, lightly beaten

1 teaspoon toasted cumin
seeds, ground (see Note,
page 123)

Salt

Freshly ground white
pepper

Olive or vegetable oil for
frying

Lemon wedges

Fried fish patties are served as a Shabbat first course among many Sephardim; an Italian variation follows.

1. Grind the fish in a food processor by pulsing just until you have a coarse mixture — don't puree. Turn it into a large mixing bowl.

2. Add the scallion or shallot, the parsley, 4 tablespoons of the bread crumbs or matzo meal, the eggs, cumin, salt, and white pepper to the fish. Mix well with your scrupulously clean hands.

3. Using a ½-tablespoon measure, form patties with the moistened palms of your hands. Flatten them slightly to about 1½ inches in diameter.

4. Heat ¼ to ½ inch of oil in a skillet.

5. Dredge the fish patties in the remaining bread crumbs or matzo meal and fry, in batches, until crisp. Serve immediately, or serve at room temperature, with lemon wedges.

VARIATION:
Instead of cumin, add a pinch of nutmeg, 1 tablespoon minced garlic, and 2 or 3 anchovy fillets to the fish.

AHEAD OF TIME NOTE:
You can prepare the dish up to the frying a day in advance. Cover and refrigerate. In fact, the frying is somewhat easier if the patties have been refrigerated for a few hours. They are best served hot, from the skillet; they are good at room temperature; they are least successful if refrigerated after frying.

FISH WITH WALNUT SAUCE

This complex walnut sauce, *tarator,* as the Turks call it, is made with walnuts by the Sephardim of Salonika, Greece, and in Turkey. In Egypt the sauce was made with pine nuts. The fish is served cold, as a first or main course. The sauce is also delicious with cold chicken and steamed vegetables.

1. In a skillet, cover the fish with water; add the parsley, onion, and lemon. Bring the liquid to a simmer and cook the fish for 5 to 10 minutes, until it is opaque and cooked through. With a flat perforated skimmer, carefully transfer the fish to a platter; don't discard the poaching liquid.

2. Soak the bread in the wine vinegar for just 2 to 3 minutes. Squeeze lightly to expel some of the liquid. Place the bread in the bowl of a food processor along with the walnuts, garlic, and olive oil. Process until you have a thick, creamy sauce. If necessary, thin the sauce with a little of the fish poaching liquid. Add salt and pepper to taste.

3. Drain off any liquid that accumulates on the fish platter. Spread the sauce over the fish and refrigerate until ready to serve, up to 5 or 6 hours, and at least 1 hour. Sprinkle with parsley before serving.

NOTE:

The sauce is assertive, so you can use such full-flavored fish as bluefish. Cod, halibut, and flounder are also good.

2 pounds fish fillets (see Note)

Several parsley sprigs

½ onion

2 thin slices lemon

2 slices day-old white bread, crusts removed

2 tablespoons red-wine vinegar

1 cup (4 ounces) walnuts

5 or 6 garlic cloves, peeled and chopped

6 tablespoons olive oil

Salt

Freshly ground black pepper

4 tablespoons minced parsley

FLOUNDER AND SALMON TERRINE

Vegetable oil

2 pounds flounder or halibut fillets

1 pound salmon fillets

4 large onions

4 large eggs

6 tablespoons matzo meal

Salt

Freshly ground white pepper

2 tablespoons lemon juice

2 carrots, grated

Parsley

Dill sprigs

Horseradish

Here's a variation on gefilte fish: it's cooked in the oven in a bain-marie rather than poached in liquid, so it's served without the traditional jellied broth. But it's a festive dish, good, too, for a light luncheon.

1. Preheat the oven to 325 degrees. Lightly oil a 2-quart loaf pan.

2. Skin and cube the fish, removing any small bones you feel. In batches, for about 10 seconds each, grind the fish in a food processor. The fish should be finely ground but not a puree.

3. Put the fish in the mixing bowl of a standing electric mixer or other large bowl. Cut the onion in eighths and mince them in the food processor. You should have about 3 cups.

4. Add the onions, eggs, matzo meal, salt, pepper, and lemon juice to the mixing bowl. Beat at medium speed for 5 to 8 minutes. You can do this with a hand beater if you don't have a standing mixer. Add the grated carrots. Combine well.

5. Place the fish mixture in the prepared loaf pan. Cover it with foil and place the loaf pan in a larger pan filled with hot water; the water should come halfway up the sides of the loaf pan.

6. Bake the fish for about 1 hour — the terrine should be firm. Let it cool for 10 minutes. Run a knife around the edge of the pan before inverting the terrine on a serving plate.

7. Refrigerate for several hours or overnight. Serve, sliced, garnished with parsley and dill sprigs. Serve with horse-radish.

GEFILTE FISH

Along with chicken soup and matzo balls, gefilte fish is the most identifiable dish of the Ashkenazic kitchen. *Gefilte* means "stuffed" in Yiddish, and these dumplings are a variation on the medieval German method of skinning and boning a fish, preparing a forcemeat, and stuffing it back into the fish skin. This technique suited the poor eastern European housewife because precious fresh fish could be stretched to feed the entire family. It also allowed the pious to conform to the rabbinic prohibition against work, which many thought included dealing with bones.

Though rarely stuffed back into fish skin, gefilte fish was one of the preeminent immigrant "best" dishes. It retains its place of importance in Jewish cooking. When my stepfather was courting my mother, her charm and beauty were greatly enhanced in his eyes by her matchless gefilte fish (which on that particular occasion was actually made by one of my mother's sisters, my dear Aunt Etta—but we never told). When I was taken to a family meal by a friend, his mother served the pride of her repertoire — gefilte fish. I hesitated over its sweet taste and she, worried and startled, asked me if I was indeed Jewish! Polish Jews use sugar in their fish; Russian Jews don't. And that's only one of many variations. Some people use carp, for color and texture; some use only whitefish and pike. Jews in the American West use salmon (see page 80); in Britain, gefilte fish is made mostly of cod, haddock, hake, and sometimes mackerel. In Israel, carp is widely used, in combination with other fish. This version is the one my friend Johanna Hecht Sokolov makes for our shared Passovers. It was her mother's recipe and it's delicious.

1. Wash the fish heads, bones, and other trimmings. Place them in a large, wide pot with 1 of the quartered onions, 2 of the sliced carrots, 2 or 3 tablespoons of the salt, pepper, and enough cold water to cover. Bring the water to boiling, reduce the heat, and simmer, partially covered, for at least 1 hour.

Ingredients

- 4 to 5 pounds fish trimmings: all the bones and heads you can coax from your fishmonger
- 3 onions, peeled and quartered
- 6 carrots, scraped and sliced
- 4 to 5 tablespoons salt
  Freshly ground black or white pepper
- 2 pounds whitefish fillets
- 2 pounds pike fillets
- 1 pound carp fillets
- ¼ cup matzo meal
- 3 eggs, lightly beaten
  About ¼ cup water
  Horseradish, red or white, or both

(continued on next page)

2. Meanwhile, coarsely grind the fillets with the remaining 2 onions in a meat grinder or food processor. Transfer the mixture to a wooden bowl and chop with a mezzaluna, or place the fish on a cutting board and chop with a knife. While you're chopping, work in 2 tablespoons of salt, the matzo meal, eggs, and water to produce a smooth mixture.

3. When the broth has cooked for at least 1 hour, strain it and discard the contents of the strainer. Put the broth in a clean pot — a large Dutch oven is best — with the remaining 4 carrots. Simmer the broth while you form the fish balls.

4. Moisten your hands with cold water and form balls or ovals about the size of golf balls or eggs. Keep a kettle of water simmering, in case you need it for the poaching.

5. Drop the fish balls, one by one, into the simmering broth, regulating the heat so the broth barely simmers. Cook the gefilte fish for 1 to 1½ hours, adding boiling water from the kettle to keep the balls floating. The gefilte fish is done when the balls feel firm to the touch. Let them cool in the broth.

6. Remove the gefilte fish with a slotted spoon to a deep serving platter. Strain the cooking liquid; reserve the carrots. Pour the liquid into a large jar and refrigerate until cold. It should gel. Refrigerate the fish and liquid separately until both are thoroughly chilled.

7. To serve, surround the fish with the gelled broth and garnish with the sliced cooked carrots. Serve with horseradish.

AHEAD OF TIME NOTE:
The gefilte fish will keep refrigerated for 3 or 4 days.

GRAVLAX

Cured salmon is a specialty of Sweden, where it was placed in the ground to keep it through the long winter. Hence the name, which means "salmon from the grave" in Swedish. To make sure they had something to eat in times of scarcity, Jews in eastern Europe used many techniques to preserve fish — they smoked, pickled, salted, and dried what fish they had. Salmon was not available in the shtetl, but here farmed salmon is ubiquitous and perfect for this dish. It's wonderful as a first course for Friday night or part of Saturday's meals. It's a great party dish, too.

¼ cup kosher salt

¼ cup sugar

2 tablespoons white peppercorns, crushed

2 center-cut salmon fillets (3 pounds) with skin (see Note)

2 large bunches dill
Mustard Sauce (see page 78)
Lemon wedges

1. In a small bowl, combine the salt, sugar, and peppercorns.

2. Rub the skin and flesh of the salmon fillets with the spice mixture. Feel for bones as you do this and remove them. Place 1 fillet on a glass or ceramic platter, skin side down. Place the bunches of dill on top of the spice mixture and cover with the other piece of salmon, skin side up. Slip the salmon into a sealable plastic bag, close it, and weight the salmon with a skillet filled with canned food or a brick. Refrigerate for 48 to 72 hours, turning the bag every 12 hours or so. The plastic bag makes the turning slightly easier, as you don't have to wrap and unwrap the salmon or deal with the liquid the fish will give up.

3. When the salmon is cured, remove the fish from its marinade and place it on paper towels. Scrape away the dill and seasoning and pat the fish dry with the paper towels. Place the separated halves, skin side down, on a board, and slice the salmon thinly on the diagonal, almost parallel to the skin. Remove any bones you encounter. Place the slices in overlapping layers on a platter. Serve as an appetizer with Mustard Sauce and lemon wedges.

NOTE:

Ask the fishmonger to slice the thick center fillet in half, removing the backbone and the smaller bones as well. If you buy the fillets already packaged, try to buy them roughly the same size.

MUSTARD SAUCE

Makes 2 cups

8 tablespoons Dijon
mustard

2 tablespoons dry mustard

6 tablespoons sugar

4 tablespoons white
vinegar

⅔ cup olive or vegetable oil

½ cup snipped dill

In a bowl, combine the mustards, sugar, and vinegar. Slowly whisk in the oil until the sauce is emulsified and as thick as mayonnaise. Add the dill. Covered and refrigerated, the sauce will keep for a couple of days. Whisk before serving.

HALIBUT IN EGG-LEMON SAUCE

Egg-lemon sauce *(avgolomeno)* is a popular preparation in Greece and Turkey. This variation on the standard is a favorite first course among eastern Mediterranean Jews.

1. Lay the halibut in a skillet large enough to accommodate it in one snug layer. Add 3 tablespoons of the lemon juice, the parsley sprigs, olive oil, and water to just cover (about 1½ cups). Season with salt and white pepper. Bring to boiling, lower the heat, and simmer very gently for 4 to 5 minutes, until barely done. Let the fish cool in the pan for a few minutes. With a large slotted skimmer, transfer the halibut to a board. Remove the skin and put it back in the poaching liquid. Cut the fish into bite-size pieces, feeling for bones as you do this. Put any you find in the poaching liquid. Place the fish on a deep serving dish. Boil the broth for about 5 minutes, until it has reduced slightly, which will intensify its flavor. Strain the liquid. Rinse the skillet and pour the liquid back into it.

2. Beat the eggs with the remaining 5 tablespoons of lemon juice. Beat in ½ cup of the warm broth. Pour the egg mixture into the skillet. Stir over very low heat for about 15 minutes, until the mixture thickens; don't boil. Stir in a pinch of turmeric for color and to intensify the lemon flavor. You should have about 1½ cups of liquid.

3. Pour the sauce over the fish. If there are any lumps in the sauce (caused by boiling), pass it through a fine sieve as you pour it over the fish; leave the lumps in the sieve, don't mash them through. Serve immediately, sprinkled with the dill, or cool, cover, refrigerate, and serve cold.

NOTE:
The easiest way to mince dill is to use scissors to cut the feathery fronds from their stalks into a small bowl.

- 2 1-pound halibut steaks, about 1 inch thick
- 8 tablespoons lemon juice
- 4 parsley sprigs
- 2 tablespoons olive oil
  Salt
  Freshly ground white pepper
- 2 eggs
  Pinch of turmeric
- 3 tablespoons minced dill (see Note)

SALMON GEFILTE FISH

1 6- to 7-pound salmon, skinned and filleted, head, and bones reserved (see Note)

6 onions, peeled and quartered

2 tablespoons kosher salt

2 teaspoons freshly ground white pepper

5 carrots, scraped and coarsely chopped

4 large eggs, lightly beaten

¼ cup matzo meal

Lettuce leaves

Horseradish

Farmed salmon has made this fish widely available and affordable. These dumplings or quenelles are a nice, pale color and an interesting and delicious alternative to classic gefilte fish. Gefilte fish is usually considered a first course, but it's delicious for lunch, too.

1. Slip a paring knife between the flesh and the skin of the salmon and gently separate the two, using a sawing motion. Put the skin, bones, and head of the salmon in a large pot (an 8- or 9-quart Dutch oven is perfect) with 3 of the quartered onions, 1 tablespoon of the salt, 1 teaspoon of the white pepper, and the carrots. Cover with 4 quarts of water and bring to boiling. Reduce heat, partially cover the pot, and simmer at least 1 hour or up to 2 to 3 hours. From time to time, skim the foam that rises to the surface of the liquid.

2. Cut the salmon into cubes, checking each piece for any bones that may remain. Grind the salmon cubes in a food processor, using the metal blade and pulsing to get the right texture — tiny pieces, not a puree. It should look like it's been chopped in a bowl with a mezzaluna, which is an alternative way to do this. Transfer the fish to a large mixing bowl.

3. Add the remaining 3 quartered onions to the work bowl of the processor. Finely chop the onions and add them to the fish along with the eggs, the matzo meal, and the remaining salt and pepper. Stir just to combine.

4. With moistened hands, make oval dumplings, using ¼ cup of the fish mixture for each. Place the dumplings on a platter and refrigerate for at least 30 minutes or up to 2 hours.

5. Gently drop the fish balls into the simmering liquid. You can easily do this with a long-handled skimmer. Don't crowd the pan — if necessary, make the fish in batches, keeping the waiting ones in the refrigerator. Cover the pot and poach the fish dumplings at a quiet simmer for about 30 minutes, until they are firm and cooked. They will rise to the top of the liquid as they cook. With a slotted spoon, transfer the fish to a deep platter or wide bowl. Add more

dumplings to the simmering liquid. When all the fish is cooked, bring the stock to boiling. Reduce it to about 2 cups. Pass the stock through a very fine sieve and strain it over the fish. Let the fish cool, then refrigerate it until cold, at least 4 hours, or preferably overnight, to give the liquid enough time to gel.

6. To serve, place 2 fish balls on a lettuce leaf for each serving. Serve with red and/or white horseradish.

NOTE:

If you cannot find a whole salmon, substitute 3 to 4 pounds of salmon fillets and the heads and bones from 2 salmon; take as much as your fishmonger will give you — the more bones, the more firmly the stock will set into a gel.

AHEAD OF TIME NOTE:

The gefilte fish will keep for 2 days, refrigerated.

1½ pounds potatoes

½ pound parsnips

¾ pound turnips

2 cups diced onion

6 tablespoons olive oil
  Salt
  Freshly ground black
  pepper

4 6- to 8-ounce salmon
  fillets

½ cup minced parsley
  Lemon wedges

SALMON WITH ROASTED VEGETABLES

These winter vegetables stand up well to the salmon, and vice versa. This is a good choice for a winter meatless meal.

1. Preheat the oven to 450 degrees.

2. Peel and dice the potatoes (about 3 cups), parsnips (1 cup), and turnips (2 cups).

3. Toss the diced vegetables with the onion and the oil in a roasting pan large enough to accommodate the vegetables in one layer.

4. Roast the vegetables for 45 to 60 minutes, tossing from time to time. They should be very soft, with patches of brown. Toss with salt and pepper.

5. Lay the salmon over the vegetables and roast for 8 to 12 minutes, depending on the thickness of the fillets. Sprinkle the salmon with parsley and serve garnished with lemon wedges.

AHEAD OF TIME NOTE:
You can make this dish 3 to 4 hours before serving, through step 4. Reheat it in the oven before adding the fish.

SALT COD IN TOMATO SAUCE

Though Italy is surrounded by water yielding lots of fresh fish, Italians love *baccala,* which Venetian traders probably brought back from Scandinavia. Baccala is cod that has been salted and dried; its close relative, *stoccafiso,* is air cured and not salted at all. Jewish merchants are thought to have brought a lot of New World foods to Italy, and this combination of salt cod and tomatoes is considered by many Italians to be a Jewish dish.

- 2 pounds baccala (dried salt cod)
- 2 cups minced onion
- 2 tablespoons sliced garlic
- 1 cup olive oil
- 1 cup white wine
- 3 cups peeled, seeded, and chopped tomatoes, fresh or canned (see Note, page 84)
- ½ cup minced parsley
- Salt
- Freshly ground black pepper
- All-purpose flour for dredging
- Grated lemon peel
- Lemon wedge

1. Soak the baccala in water to cover for 24 to 48 hours, changing the water at least every 12 hours.

2. On the day you plan to serve the cod, sauté the onion and garlic in 2 tablespoons of the olive oil until very tender but not brown, about 20 minutes. Add the wine, bring to boiling, and immediately add the tomatoes and all but a small handful of the parsley. Cook rapidly, mashing with a wooden spoon, until you have a thick sauce. Add more wine, water, or liquid from the canned tomatoes if the sauce is sticking. Add salt and pepper to taste. Pass the sauce through a food mill back into the skillet. The sauce will lavishly coat the bottom of a 10-inch skillet.

3. Drain the salt cod on paper towels. Break it into 2- to 3-inch pieces, picking out any bones you encounter.

4. Spread some flour on a plate and dredge the cod pieces in it, shaking to remove the excess.

5. Heat the remaining oil in a large skillet. When the oil is almost smoking, fry the cod in batches, without crowding the pan, until golden. Drain on paper towels.

6. Before serving, reheat the tomato sauce; add the cod and just heat through. Just before serving, garnish with the grated lemon peel, the reserved parsley, and the lemon wedges.

(continued on next page)

If you use canned tomatoes for the sauce, add a little tomato paste — just 1 or 2 teaspoons.

AHEAD OF TIME NOTE:
You can make this dish a few hours ahead of time through step 5. Don't refrigerate the cod, because it will lose texture and interest.

STRIPED BASS WITH LENTILS

Serves 5 or 6 as a main course, or 8 or 9 as a first course

This elegant yet hearty combination is flavorful, and much of it can be prepared in advance.

1. In a saucepan, combine the lentils, broth, garlic cloves, wine vinegar, and bay leaf. Bring to boiling, lower the heat, and simmer, covered, for 40 minutes, or until the lentils are tender but not mushy. If you are completing the dish at this point, drain any liquid remaining with the lentils. If you wait, the lentils will absorb the liquid. Discard the bay leaf and squeeze the garlic cloves to release their pulp. Keep the lentils covered until ready to use. Reheat very gently, adding more water if necessary.

2. Preheat the oven to 400 degrees.

3. Wash and dry the fillets. Brush each fillet with olive oil and season it with salt and pepper. Roast the fish in an uncovered roasting pan for 8 to 15 minutes, depending on the thickness of the fillets.

4. Spread the lentils on a platter and place the fish over them. Sprinkle with parsley and serve.

NOTE:
The lentils are delicious without the fish, too. Serve as a side dish.

1 cup lentils

2 cups vegetable broth or water

5 or 6 unpeeled garlic cloves

1 tablespoon wine vinegar

1 bay leaf

4 8-ounce fillets of striped bass, blackfish, cod, or other white, firm-fleshed fish

1 tablespoon olive oil

Salt

Freshly ground black pepper

¼ cup chopped parsley

STUFFED RED SNAPPER

1 whole red snapper (or one of the suggested fish), 3 to 4 pounds, cleaned

Salt

FOR THE STUFFING:

4 eggs: 2 hard-boiled (see Note, page 38), 2 raw, lightly beaten

¾ cup bread crumbs

½ cup slivered almonds

¼ cup minced parsley

⅓ teaspoon grated nutmeg

2 tablespoons olive oil

½ cup thinly sliced onion

6 garlic cloves, peeled and minced

1 lemon, finely sliced and pitted

8 to 10 cherry tomatoes, halved

4 bay leaves

⅛ teaspoon pulverized saffron

3 tablespoons olive oil

This stuffed fish from Morocco is good both hot and cold and can be enjoyed as an entrée or appetizer. It makes an impressive presentation. Other good fish for this dish are mullet, grouper, and sea perch.

1. Wash the fish inside and out. Dry the fish and lightly salt the interior.

2. Mash the hard-boiled eggs in a mixing bowl with a fork. Add the bread crumbs, almonds, parsley, nutmeg, oil, and raw eggs. Stir to combine.

3. Preheat the oven to 400 degrees.

4. Stuff the fish with the bread-crumb mixture. Close the opening with skewers. Place the fish in a shallow ovenproof dish in which it just fits. If your dish isn't long enough to accommodate the fish, wrap the tail in aluminum foil.

5. Scatter the onion, garlic, lemon, tomatoes, bay leaves, and saffron over the fish. Salt it lightly and sprinkle it with oil. Pour a cup of water into the bottom of the dish and cook the fish in the preheated oven for 30 to 45 minutes, until the fish is just done. Baste from time to time.

6. Let the fish cool for 10 to 15 minutes. Carefully transfer it to a platter. Slit it down the back from head to tail. Remove the stuffing to a bowl. Gently lift out the bone, leaving the fish intact for an impressive presentation. You can replace the stuffing in the fish or serve it from the bowl. Surround the fish with the vegetables and cooking juices, discarding the bay leaves. To serve cold, cool the fish to room temperature, then cover lightly and refrigerate it for up to several hours.

POULTRY

If a poor man eats chicken,
one of them is sick.

YIDDISH PROVERB

THERE IS EVIDENCE THAT THE
Roman legions introduced the chicken into Europe
from the Near East. Though in Europe during the
Middle Ages the chicken was a scrawny and unappeal-
ing creature, in Egypt it thrived. John Cooper, in
his excellent book *Eat and Be Satisfied,* tells us that
Maimonides (1135–1204) repeated the wisdom of his
teacher, Abu Merwan ibn Zohar, who regarded fowl
and chicken soup as beneficial to the sick. So that tradition goes way back.

The recipes in this chapter vary widely in their
origin: American Chicken Pie, a Persian tabyit, French
Coq au Vin. The chapter illustrates the diverse influ-
ences on Jewish cooking in this country and reflects the
almost universal Jewish consumption of chicken on
Friday night.

ROAST CHICKEN

This is the traditional Shabbos dinner of my childhood. Chicken was very expensive in eastern Europe and therefore a suitable special meal. Here it is inexpensive, but the tradition persists.

This is a simple and delicious preparation. If you have more or less of the listed ingredients, that's okay; if you want to add a turnip or a parsnip, that would be good, too. It's forgiving in its proportions, but be careful not to overcook the chicken. If you don't want the vegetables, just roast the chicken on a rack, stuffed with the lemon, a quartered onion, and rosemary.

3 large russet potatoes
4 or 5 carrots
3 large onions
Salt
Freshly ground black pepper
Olive oil
1 4- to 5-pound chicken
1 lemon, quartered
Large sprig fresh rosemary or parsley

1. Preheat the oven to 450 degrees.

2. Cut the potatoes into quarters or eighths and place them in a large saucepan with cold water to cover. Bring to boiling, reduce the heat, and simmer for about 10 minutes — the potatoes should be barely tender. Remove them to a bowl with a slotted spoon and keep the water boiling.

3. Slice the carrots into chunks. Parboil them for 5 minutes or so in the water in which you boiled the potatoes. Drain and place them in a large, heavy roasting pan.

4. Cut the onions in half and slice the halves thinly. Place them in the pan with the carrots.

5. When the potatoes are cool enough to handle, peel them and cut them into large dice. Place them in the roasting pan with the onions and carrots. Add salt and pepper; sprinkle with olive oil. Stir the vegetables to combine and distribute the seasonings and oil.

6. Stuff the chicken with the lemon quarters and rosemary or parsley. Put the chicken on top of the vegetables and place the pan in the preheated oven. Roast the chicken for about 1 hour — the juices should run clear and the drumstick should be flexible in its joint. Remove the chicken and set it aside on a carving board for about 10 minutes. Stir the vegetables and put them back in the oven until you've carved the chicken. Serve them on the platter with the carved chicken, or in a vegetable dish.

1 4- to 5-pound chicken
(see Note)

3 tablespoons olive oil

4 tablespoons Dijon
mustard

3 tablespoons minced
shallot

4 tablespoons minced
parsley

Hot sauce

1 cup bread crumbs

BROILED BUTTERFLIED CHICKEN WITH MUSTARD COATING

This unusual-looking presentation is very impressive. The chicken, with its backbone removed, is splayed out whole, coated with an appealingly golden bread-crumb crust. I learned this recipe many years ago from an early Julia Child book.

1. Split the chicken by removing the backbone with a sharp knife. To make the chicken lie flat, place it breast up on a board and bang it with your fist or a mallet. Wash and dry the chicken.

2. Preheat the broiler and place a rack about 6 inches from the heat.

3. Brush the chicken on both sides with some of the oil. Place it on the broiler rack and grill it for 5 minutes. Brush a little more oil on the chicken if it looks dry. Raise the heat or the broiler rack and cook for 5 more minutes. Turn the chicken, brush with more oil, and broil for 10 more minutes, checking once to make sure the chicken isn't burning.

4. Combine the mustard, shallot, parsley, a few drops of hot sauce, and 1 tablespoon of the olive oil.

5. Spread the underside of the chicken with the mustard mixture; sprinkle on half of the bread crumbs. Drizzle a little oil on and replace the chicken, skin side down, on the broiler rack. Broil for 5 minutes.

6. Using two large wooden spoons or spatulas, remove the chicken and place it skin side up on a large board. This is the trickiest part of the recipe because the chicken is a little wobbly and you'll lose some bread crumbs on the board. The wooden implements will provide a good grip and give you assurance. Coat the skin side with the remaining mustard mixture, pat on the remaining bread crumbs, and drizzle with the remaining olive oil. Replace the chicken under the broiler and grill for 5 final minutes.

7. Bring the whole chicken to the table on a board and carve it as you serve.

NOTE:

You can substitute a cut-up chicken for the butterflied one — it will taste delicious but won't look quite so grand.

Serves 5 or 6

1 4½- to 5-pound chicken,
cut in eighths

2 tablespoons olive oil

4 or 5 medium carrots,
scraped

1 large green pepper

1 cup sliced onion

1 tablespoon sliced garlic

1 cup canned tomatoes

⅓ cup liquid from the
tomatoes

1 cup uncooked white rice

1½ cups chicken stock

1 2-inch piece orange peel
(removed with a swivel-
bladed vegetable peeler)

Salt

Freshly ground black
pepper

CASSEROLE OF CHICKEN AND RICE

This rich combination makes an excellent one-pot meal.

1. Wash and dry the chicken pieces.

2. Heat the oil in a large skillet and sauté the chicken pieces, in one layer, for 5 minutes or so on each side, until they turn golden. You'll probably need to do this in batches, though the skillet must be large enough to hold all the ingredients. As each batch is done, remove the pieces to a plate.

3. While the chicken is browning, prepare the vegetables. Cut the carrots in half and slice each half, lengthwise, into thin strips. Wash, seed, and thinly slice the green pepper.

4. Add the onion and garlic to the skillet, scraping the bottom of the skillet with a wooden spoon to dislodge the brown bits. Sauté for a few minutes, just until the onion softens. Add the tomatoes, their juice, the rice, the stock, and the orange peel; season with salt and pepper. Stir well. Replace the chicken pieces, reserving the breast pieces. Bring to a simmer, cover the skillet, and cook slowly for 10 minutes. Add the breast pieces and cook for another 20 to 30 minutes, until the chicken is tender and the rice is done. Transfer to a platter and serve.

AHEAD OF TIME NOTE:

The cooking can be interrupted and resumed almost anywhere along the way. The dish can be completed in advance and reheated gently over a flame-tamer.

CHICKEN
"BALABUSTA"

I've taken liberties here with the French preparation "Bonne Femme," which means a simply cooked dish as prepared by the "good housewife" (*balabusta,* in Yiddish) in a cocotte, or oval casserole dish. The chicken cooks in its own juices and at its best is succulent and moist. The traditional French preparation includes bacon, but the dish doesn't suffer without that authentic ingredient.

1. Wash and dry the chicken (it won't brown if it's moist). Place the rosemary in the cavity. Fold the wing tips back and truss the bird or at least tie the legs together.

2. Preheat the oven to 350 degrees.

3. Heat 4 tablespoons of the olive oil in an enameled cast-iron or tin-lined copper oval or round casserole dish with a tight-fitting lid in which the chicken and vegetables will fit snugly. Brown the chicken, starting with the breast side. Turn the chicken to its side after 5 to 6 minutes. Keep turning the chicken until it is brown on all sides — this will take about 25 to 30 minutes. With a bulb baster, remove all but a very thin film of fat.

4. While the chicken is browning, heat the remaining 2 tablespoons of olive oil in a skillet. Sauté the vegetables until they are lightly colored and glazed with oil, about 20 to 25 minutes over very low heat. Transfer the vegetables to the casserole dish with the browned chicken. Season with salt and pepper; add the parsley and bay leaf bundle, cover the casserole dish, and place it in the oven. (The chicken can also be cooked on top of the stove over very low heat.)

5. Cook the chicken for about 1 hour, basting from time to time with the accumulated juice in the pot. Remove the finished chicken to a carving board and replace the vegetables, uncovered, in the oven.

6. Carve the chicken after a 10-minute rest. Place the pieces back in the casserole dish, on top of the vegetables; sprinkle with parsley and serve.

(continued on next page)

1 4- to 5-pound chicken
  Sprig fresh rosemary or 1 teaspoon dried

6 tablespoons olive oil

2 tablespoons chopped garlic

1 pound small white onions (see Note, page 94)

6 carrots, cut into 2-inch pieces

1½ pounds potatoes, cut into 2-inch dice
  Salt
  Freshly ground black pepper

6 parsley sprigs tied with 1 bay leaf

4 tablespoons chopped parsley

NOTE:

To peel small white onions, shave the root end and cut a cross in it; peel the onion, cutting off the top.

AHEAD OF TIME NOTE:

You can sauté the vegetables several hours in advance of serving; the chicken can also be browned. To complete the cooking, combine the ingredients and heat on top of the stove before placing in the oven.

CHICKEN AND MACARONI

Though it sounds like a casserole from the 1950s, this delicious dish is a Friday-night favorite of Syrian Jews. Brooklyn has a large community of Syrians, and this recipe is inspired by one privately published by Rae Dayan, a member of that community. As the pasta bakes, it absorbs the flavors of the sauce and the chicken; perhaps best of all, the dish has a wonderful crisp crust.

1. Preheat the oven to 500 degrees (see Note, page 111).

2. Wash and dry the chicken.

3. Put the garlic through a press or mash it in a mortar with a pestle. Make a paste with the garlic, paprika, olive oil, and coarse salt. Rub the paste over the chicken; slip your fingers under the skin and spread some paste directly on the chicken flesh.

4. Scatter the onion on the bottom of a roasting pan, separating it into rings. Place the chicken on a rack over the onion, breast side up. Add ½ cup of water. Roast for 1 hour, turning once. If the chicken's juice is still pink, roast until the juice is yellow and the chicken is tender.

5. Cook the macaroni in a large quantity of boiling water. Drain.

6. Place the macaroni in a large mixing bowl. Add the tomatoes, stock, cinnamon, allspice, salt, and pepper, and combine.

7. Remove the chicken from the oven. Reduce the temperature to 400 degrees. When the chicken is cool enough to handle, slice the meat from the bones. Defat the roasting juice and the onion and combine with the macaroni-tomato mixture. Transfer to a 3-quart gratin dish. Bury the chicken pieces in the macaroni, cover the dish, and return it to the oven for 30 minutes; remove the cover and cook for an additional 15 minutes, until the top is crisp.

1 4½- to 5-pound chicken

4 large garlic cloves, peeled

1 teaspoon paprika

2 tablespoons olive oil

1 teaspoon kosher salt

2 cups thinly sliced onion

1 pound elbow macaroni

2 cups canned ground or chopped, peeled tomatoes

2 cups chicken stock

2 teaspoons ground cinnamon

½ teaspoon ground allspice
Salt
Freshly ground black pepper

CHICKEN AND RICE

1½ cups uncooked white rice

1 tablespoon vegetable oil

1 cup minced onion

1 tablespoon tomato paste

1 teaspoon ground turmeric

1 teaspoon ground cardamom

1 teaspoon ground cinnamon

1 tablespoon minced fresh ginger

½ teaspoon allspice

Pinch ground cloves

1 cup chopped fresh or canned tomatoes

Salt

Freshly ground black pepper

1 4- to 5-pound chicken, including giblets, chopped

This dish, the chicken both stuffed with rice and cooked on rice, is the typical Sabbath dish of Baghdad, though rice-and-chicken dishes were common throughout the Levant. Claudia Roden, in her illuminating book *The Book of Jewish Food,* explains that this dish was cooked in a wide-bottomed, narrow-necked cauldron that sat on a brazier and heated slowly in the embers of Friday-night's fire. Eggs, placed on the lid, cooked in the steam, their creamy texture and delicious taste a welcome-home treat for the men returning from synagogue on Saturday morning.

At lunchtime on Saturday, the pot was placed in cold water to help unstick the rice. When it was turned out on a platter, it resembled a large cake, with the chicken inside. Try as I might (and I tried several times), I have never achieved this. The dish is delicious — redolent of Middle Eastern flavors, but moist and not cakelike, with only a little crunchy rice on the bottom. Nowadays, modern ovens and cooktops allow us to cook the dish quickly, and *tabyit,* as this dish is called, is often served for Friday dinner.

1. Bring 1 quart of water to boiling. Add the rice, cover the pot, and let the rice soak for 20 minutes off the heat.

2. Heat the vegetable oil in a Dutch oven large enough to hold the chicken. Tin-lined copper and enameled cast iron are both good. Sauté the onion for a few minutes, just until softened. Add the tomato paste and all the spices, stirring to combine after each addition. Finally, add the tomatoes, including any liquid from canned tomatoes. Stir. Add the rice and 2 cups of water. Bring the rice to boiling, add salt and pepper, lower the heat, cover the pot, and simmer for 15 minutes.

3. Preheat the oven to 400 degrees.

4. Combine ½ to 1 cup of the rice mixture with the giblets. Stuff the chicken cavity about two-thirds full, allowing space for the rice to expand. Sew or skewer the chicken closed.

5. Place the chicken on top of the remaining rice, adding 1 cup of water. Place the lid on the pot, and cook the chicken for 1 hour at 400 degrees and for another hour at 225 to 250 degrees. Alternatively, you can cook the chicken overnight at 225 degrees. If you want a brown skin on the chicken, remove the lid and raise the heat in the oven for the last 15 minutes to 450 degrees.

6. To serve, place the chicken on a platter, topped and surrounded with the rice.

CHICKEN IN ESCABECHE

6 tablespoons olive oil

1½ to 2 cups thinly sliced onion

1 cup sliced carrot

1 cup sliced celery

8 to 10 garlic cloves, peeled but left whole

1½ to 2 cups sliced red, green, or yellow peppers, or a combination

1 lemon, thinly sliced

½ cup dry white wine

⅓ cup wine vinegar

½ teaspoon fresh or dried rosemary

1 bay leaf

Several parsley sprigs

4 to 6 cups chicken stock

4 to 5 pounds chicken parts: legs, thighs, breasts; or 1 6- to 7-pound chicken, cut into serving pieces; or a 7- to 8- pound fowl

Salt

Freshly ground black pepper

Lemon wedges

Escabeche is a marinade of broth, water, vinegar, wine, herbs, and spices in which fish, game, and poultry, are cooked and marinated. The flavor is piquant and lively; in addition, the escabeche preserves food. The word comes through the Spanish from the Arabic *sakbay,* meaning "pickled" or "sour." The technique is Iberian; in medieval Spain it referred to dishes made with vinegar, lemon, or sour pomegranate juice. In countries where game was popular and plentiful it was used to preserve it — partridge in escabeche is popular in Spain. Fish in escabeche is common in France. This chicken in escabeche will be popular in your house as a special and delicious summer Shabbat dinner. It's all made in advance, on Wednesday or Thursday if you like.

1. Heat the oil in a heavy 6-quart casserole dish. Add the onion, carrot, celery, and garlic. Cook slowly, stirring occasionally, for 15 to 20 minutes. The vegetables should soften but not color.

2. Add the sliced peppers, lemon, wine, vinegar, rosemary, bay leaf, parsley, and 4 cups of chicken stock. Bring to boiling and simmer slowly for 20 to 30 minutes.

3. Add the chicken pieces to the casserole dish along with any giblets (not the liver). Add enough additional stock or water to just cover the chicken pieces. Cover the pot, turn the heat to the lowest setting (or put the pot on a flame-tamer), and cook at the barest simmer until the chicken is just tender. The timing will vary depending on the type and size of chicken you use. For a tender young chicken, 1 hour might be enough; for a fowl, 2 or 3 hours is more likely. Test the chicken — you want it tender but not falling off the bone. And don't forget, it will continue to cook in the hot liquid as it cools.

4. Let the chicken cool in the liquid for at least 1 hour. With a slotted spoon, remove the chicken pieces to a deep platter along with the vegetables and lemon slices. After the large pieces are removed, strain the rest into a bowl. It should then be easy to find and discard the bay leaf, parsley, and giblets, as well as any loose bones. Skim as much fat off the liquid as you can. If you have the time, put the liquid in the freezer for a couple of hours; the fat will harden on the top and be easy to remove.

5. Boil down the liquid until it is reduced to 2½ to 3 cups. Add salt and pepper to taste. Pour the liquid over the chicken. Cool to room temperature before refrigerating, covered, for at least 6 hours. The sauce will thicken and gel — a perfect summer dinner. Serve garnished with lemon wedges.

CHICKEN PIE

3 cups thinly sliced onion

2 tablespoons minced garlic

3 tablespoons olive or vegetable oil

4 tablespoons flour

2 to 2½ cups hot chicken stock

Salt

Freshly ground black pepper

Hot sauce

2 cups diced carrot (about 6 medium)

1 cup diced parsnip (about 3 medium)

5 to 6 cups cubed cooked chicken

4 cups diced cooked potato (1½ pounds)

1 cup cooked fresh peas or still-frozen peas

1 cup fresh or still-frozen corn

1 pound frozen pareve puff pastry, refrigerated for 2 hours before using

1 egg, lightly beaten

Here's a satisfying and festive way to use the chicken yielded from chicken soup. If you don't have leftover chicken, poach parts or a whole five- to six-pound chicken with a quartered onion and a couple of scraped, quartered carrots; save the broth and use it the next time you make chicken soup. Choice of vegetables is flexible; this combination offers color, texture, and taste contrasts. But make substitutions or deletions according to your preference.

1. Preheat the oven to 400 degrees. Oil a 3½-quart gratin dish.

2. Sauté the onion and garlic in the oil slowly until the onion softens, about 15 minutes.

3. Stir in the flour and then the hot stock. Heat to simmering. Cook, stirring, until the sauce thickens. Add salt, pepper, and hot sauce to taste.

4. Cook the carrot and parsnip in a large quantity of boiling water for about 5 minutes. Drain.

5. Combine the sauce with the chicken and all the vegetables. Transfer the chicken-vegetable mixture to the prepared dish.

6. About 45 minutes before you plan to serve the pie, roll out the pastry to fit over your dish with an inch or so overhang. Gently drape the pastry over the pie dish. Roll the pin over the top of the pie dish and the excess pastry will fall away. You can decorate the top with cutouts, made freehand or with cookie cutters, from the excess pastry. Make sure you make a few air holes with a fork. Brush the pastry with the beaten egg.

7. Bake the pie in the preheated oven for about 40 minutes. The pastry should be golden and the pie more or less set.

AHEAD OF TIME NOTE:

You can make the pie in advance through step 5. Bring the chicken-vegetable mixture to a simmer on top of the stove before covering it with pastry and baking.

CHICKEN WITH POMEGRANATE, NUTS, AND RICE

Jewish tradition says that pomegranates have as many seeds as the number of mitzvoth the pious are obligated to perform. This festive dish, Middle Eastern in origin, uses pomegranate syrup; decorate it with pomegranate seeds, though all 613 mitzvoth needn't be represented in this one dish.

1. Preheat the oven to 350 degrees.

2. Stuff the chicken with the lemon and the parsley sprigs. Place it on a rack in a roasting pan. Sprinkle the chicken with salt and pepper and brush with the pomegranate syrup mixture. Roast the chicken for 1½ hours, basting every few minutes with the pomegranate syrup mixture; turn once.

3. Start the rice dish after the chicken has cooked for 30 minutes. Heat the oil in a saucepan and add the pine nuts, stirring until they turn color. Be careful: they quickly turn from golden to burned. Remove the nuts with a slotted spoon and drain on paper towels. Add the almonds to the oil, stirring until they turn golden. Drain them on paper towels. Add the lamb to the pan, stirring until it loses its pink color and pressing it against the sides of the pan to break up lumps. Carefully holding back the lamb with a spoon, pour off as much liquid as you can from the pan; don't risk losing any meat — just pour off what's easy.

4. Stir the raw rice into the lamb, along with the nuts. Pour in the chicken stock and stir in the cinnamon, allspice, and additional salt and pepper. Bring to boiling, reduce the heat, cover, and cook for 15 to 20 minutes, until the rice is done, stirring once or twice. Turn off the heat. To absorb any remaining moisture, remove cover, drape a kitchen towel over pan, and replace cover. Set aside while you finish preparing the dish.

(continued on next page)

1 4-pound chicken

1 lemon, quartered

A few parsley sprigs

Salt

Freshly ground black pepper

2 tablespoons pomegranate syrup mixed with 6 tablespoons water

4 tablespoons olive oil

⅓ cup pine nuts

⅓ cup blanched whole almonds

½ pound lean ground lamb

1 cup uncooked white rice

2 cups chicken stock

½ teaspoon ground cinnamon

½ teaspoon ground allspice

2 ripe pomegranates, seeded (optional)

5. Remove the chicken to a board and let it sit for 15 minutes. Place the roasting pan over medium heat on a burner and add ½ cup of water. Scraping to dislodge the nice brown bits, bring the drippings to boiling. Boil down rapidly until the sauce is slightly thickened. Skim off any apparent fat. Pour the sauce into a sauceboat.

6. Carve the chicken. Put the rice on a platter, arrange the chicken pieces on top, sprinkle with pomegranate seeds, if using, and serve, accompanied by the gravy.

AHEAD OF TIME NOTE:

If you want to get a jump on the recipe early in the day of serving, begin at step 3 and continue through step 4, stopping after you add the chicken stock, cinnamon, allspice, salt, and pepper. Don't bring to simmering until the chicken is 20 minutes away from being ready.

ABOUT POMEGRANATES

Pomegranates are a hard-shelled fruit with bright red skin and hundreds of seeds embedded in white membranes. They have a tart-sweet flavor and a deep red juice, and are available in autumn. Pomegranates should have shiny skin with no signs of shriveling. They should be plump and feel heavy for their size. To get to the seeds, first put on an apron, and work over the sink. Peel the pomegranate by slicing off its top and base. With a serrated knife, score the rind lengthwise in several places. Pry off the skin along the scoring, being careful to remove all traces of the thick yellow skin, which is very bitter. Separate the seeds from the membranes; place them on paper towels and pat dry. Store the seeds, tightly covered, in the refrigerator for a few days, or in the freezer for many months.

MIDDLE EASTERN CHICKEN

This dish, *maqlub bi Djaj* or *Dajaaj al riz,* is often served in Syrian and Iraqi homes on Friday night. The homey dish is cooked in two steps, which makes it attractive for the busy Shabbat cook. It can all be assembled well in advance of cooking. Though delicious, it's not beautiful, so save it for the family.

1. Soak the rice in warm water to cover for 20 to 30 minutes.

2. Carve the cooked chicken into large pieces and remove the skin and bones.

3. Drain the rice and combine it with the salt, pepper, allspice, cinnamon, nuts, and drained raisins.

4. Preheat the oven to 350 degrees.

5. Place the rice in a 6- to 8-cup pie plate, gratin dish, or decorative ovenproof serving dish. Put the chicken pieces on top. Pour the stock over the chicken, cover with foil, and bake for 30 minutes or so, until the rice is cooked and the liquid is absorbed. Garnish the chicken with the parsley.

AHEAD OF TIME NOTE:

The dish can be prepared through the middle of step 5. Don't add the chicken stock until the final oven cooking. If you refrigerate it, bring it to room temperature before placing it in the oven.

1 cup uncooked white rice

1 4- to 5- pound chicken, boiled or simply roasted

Salt

Freshly ground black pepper

1 teaspoon ground allspice

½ teaspoon ground cinnamon

4 tablespoons pine nuts or blanched almonds

2 tablespoons raisins, plumped in hot water for 1 hour

2 cups chicken stock, boiling

2 tablespoons chopped parsley

CHICKEN PAPRIKASH

1 3½- to 4-pound chicken, cut into 8 pieces and including the heart, neck, back, and gizzard

Salt

Freshly ground black pepper

2 tablespoons sweet paprika

5 tablespoons vegetable oil or shmaltz (page 36)

1½ to 2 cups thinly sliced onion

1 cup chicken stock

1 red bell pepper, cut into julienne strips

3 tomatoes, seeded and peeled, fresh or canned

This Hungarian specialty has been a staple of American cooking since 1906, when a recipe for it appeared in *The Boston Cooking-School Cookbook* by Fannie Farmer. Three decades later, Mrs. Rombauer spread its fame when she published a recipe in *The Joy of Cooking*. *The Settlement Cookbook,* the cookbook that taught Jewish immigrants how to be American, offers a recipe for Chicken Paprika, but it includes milk and sour cream! This recipe has neither and is completely kosher, if not completely authentic. It's good with boiled noodles or a noodle kugel.

1. Wash and dry the chicken pieces.

2. In a small bowl, combine 1 teaspoon of salt, 1 teaspoon of pepper, and 2 teaspoons of the paprika. Rub this mixture into the chicken pieces and let it sit while you prepare the rest of the ingredients. If you have leftover salt mixture, save it for step 6.

3. Heat 4 tablespoons of the oil or shmaltz in a 12-inch sauté pan and in it brown the chicken pieces in batches so the chicken is never crowded. When the pieces are nicely colored, after about 10 minutes, remove them to a plate while you finish the remaining chicken. Leave the heart, neck, back, and gizzard in the pan, if you are using them — they give a rich quality to the finished dish.

4. Put the sliced onion in the sauté pan along with 1 teaspoon of the paprika (or leftover salt-pepper-paprika mixture from step 2 and enough additional paprika to make 1 teaspoon) and ½ cup of the chicken stock. Scrape up the bits left on the bottom of the pan, lower the heat, cover, and cook for 20 minutes, until the onion is meltingly soft.

5. Put the chicken pieces back in the pan along with the julienned pepper, tomatoes, and remaining ½ cup chicken stock. Partially cover the chicken and cook it over low heat for 30 to 40 minutes, until the chicken is done.

6. Just before the chicken is done, heat the remaining 1 tablespoon of oil or shmaltz in a small saucepan; stir in 1 teaspoon of paprika. Pour this mixture over the chicken before serving.

NOTE:

Like most chicken dishes, this reheats just fine, though it loses a little textural interest.

COQ AU VIN

2 4-pound chickens, each cut into eighths (reserve the livers)

Salt

Freshly ground black pepper

6 tablespoons olive oil

4 carrots, thickly sliced

3 cups chopped onion

4 celery stalks, thickly sliced

½ cup flour

4 garlic cloves, peeled

Bouquet garni of 1 bay leaf, 4 or 5 parsley sprigs, and celery leaves, tied in clean cheesecloth

4 cups hearty, young red wine

2 cups chicken stock

GARNISH:

30 pearl onions

2 tablespoons olive oil

1 pound small mushrooms, trimmed; quarter them, if large

Salt

Freshly ground black pepper

Minced parsley

This traditional stew of chicken and vegetables cooked in wine is a classic of French cooking. Easily adapted to the laws of kashrut, Coq au Vin is an appropriate and welcome Shabbat dish. The recipe is long and requires many steps, but it can be done in stages and in advance. It is usually served with steamed potatoes.

1. Wash the chicken pieces and pat them dry with paper towels. Season them with salt and pepper.

2. In a cast-iron skillet, heat 3 tablespoons of the olive oil. In batches, brown the chicken pieces. Turn the chicken pieces to color all sides; as they are done, transfer them to a large Dutch oven or casserole dish. Add the additional olive oil, as needed. This will take ½ hour or so.

3. Add the carrots, onion, and celery. Cook them slowly for about 15 minutes, until soft. Add the flour to the skillet, stirring until it starts to color. Stir the vegetable-flour mixture into the pot with the chicken.

4. Add the garlic cloves, bouquet garni, wine, and chicken stock. Bring to boiling, lower the heat, cover the pot, and cook very slowly for about 40 to 45 minutes, until the chicken is just done; cook for less time if you're making the chicken in advance.

5. While the chicken cooks, broil the livers and set them aside.

6. Prepare the garnishes. Shave the root end off the pearl onions. With a small sharp knife, make a cross in the root ends and peel them.

7. Heat the olive oil in a medium-size skillet. Add the onion and cook, covered, stirring from time to time, until they soften. Remove the cover and raise the heat to brown the onions. Transfer to a bowl.

8. Add the mushrooms to the skillet and sauté for 1 minute over high heat. Reduce the heat, cover the pot, and cook for a few minutes, until the mushrooms have released their juice. Raise the heat to high to evaporate the juice and color the mushrooms slightly. Transfer them to the bowl with the onions. Season with salt and pepper.

9. Remove the chicken to a platter and pass the cooking liquid through a sieve back into the casserole. Discard the contents of the sieve and the bouquet garni. Boil the liquid until it reduces slightly. Remove about ¼ cup of the liquid and place it with the reserved livers in a processor. Puree. Return the puree to the sauce, stirring it in.

10. Taste the sauce for seasoning; it should be rich, thick, and tasty. Return the chicken to the pot just long enough to heat it. Add the mushrooms and onions. Serve the Coq au Vin sprinkled with parsley.

AHEAD OF TIME NOTE:

You can make the Coq au Vin through step 9 several hours in advance. I think the taste and texture of cooked chicken are better if it hasn't been refrigerated, so don't make this more than 5 to 6 hours in advance.

CHICKEN FRICASSEE

1 4- to 5-pound chicken
   (including giblets),
   cut up
4 tablespoons vegetable oil
4 cups chopped onion
1 teaspoon tomato paste
2 cups chopped canned
   tomato, with 1 cup of the
   tomato liquid
   Salt
   Freshly ground black
   pepper

MEATBALLS:

1 pound ground beef
1 egg
1 tablespoon minced garlic
   Salt
   Freshly ground black
   pepper

When I asked my old friend Harvey Levenstein, a historian born and bred in Toronto, what he had eaten on Friday evening in his mother's kosher home, he answered quickly and without hesitation, "Fricassee." He talked to his brother and to his friend Louis Greenspan, and though the three of them couldn't come up with a precise recipe, Harvey's description was vivid. "Louis's mother, the *rebbetzin,* did exactly what mine did: served fricassee as a *vorspeis,* before the chicken soup. It consisted of the gizzard, neck, and sometimes little meatballs, in a bit of broth, which was sopped up with fresh challah. It was served in little dishes that looked like soup bowls, except one-third the size. My guess is that it was made by frying up some onions (an essential ingredient) and, as they were browning, adding the gizzard, neck, and optional meatballs, browning them briefly, and then adding water to cover and half a ton of salt. It would then be cooked for the usual twelve hours that one cooked all meats. Sometimes my mother would add tiny matzo balls — that might have been on Pesach, or when she felt particularly creative, I forget when — but it was not part of the standard recipe." Our friend Neal Goldman remembers the same dish in his mother's kosher home in Newark, but with less relish. It's a good guess that few Jewish housewives knew that "fricassee" is a French method of preparing poultry in a white sauce and that it used to apply to meat, fish, and vegetables as well as poultry.

For the Jewish housewife, fricassee was the ultimate thrifty dish: every part of the bird was used. The hen was boiled for the all-important soup, but the least desirable parts — feet, beak, gizzard, neck — were saved for a fricassee. Harvey's mother's gravy got its body from these gelatin-yielding parts. Nowadays it's harder and more expensive to get the beaks and feet than the ubiquitous legs, thighs, wings, and breasts. If you can get feet, they add wonderful texture to the sauce. This New World version is one my mother made often; it even includes tomatoes, which certainly weren't available to her Old-World-eastern-European mother. Serve with rice or noodles or boiled potatoes.

1. Wash the chicken and dry the pieces on paper towels.

2. Heat the oil in a large, deep skillet or Dutch oven with a tight-fitting lid. In batches, brown the chicken pieces on all sides in the hot oil. As the pieces are done, remove them to a platter to make room in the pot for more.

3. When all the chicken is brown, add the onion to the skillet. Cook slowly, until the onion is soft and lightly colored. Stir in the tomato paste and the tomato and tomato liquid. Add the chicken pieces and the giblets (though not the liver). The liquid should partially cover the chicken. Add salt and pepper, bring the liquid to simmering, and cover the pot. Cook at a gentle simmer for 20 minutes.

4. To make the meatballs, combine the beef, egg, garlic, salt, and pepper in a large bowl. Mix well. Form small meatballs using a scant tablespoon of the mixture for each ball. Use moistened hands to roll them. Add the meatballs to the chicken, re-cover the pot, and simmer for an additional 20 minutes. Remove the chicken to a platter; surround it with the meatballs. Taste the sauce for seasoning and reduce it over high heat, if necessary, to intensify its flavor.

AHEAD OF TIME NOTE:

If you have time, remove the chicken and meatballs and strain the liquid. Refrigerate it to allow the fat to rise to the top and, if you have a lot of time, harden, to make removal easier. Remove what fat you can. Reheat and serve.

PIQUANT CHICKEN GRATIN

½ cup minced shallot

2 tablespoons minced garlic

4 tablespoons olive oil or vegetable oil

3 tablespoons wine vinegar

1 cup peeled, seeded, and chopped tomato, fresh or canned

1 tablespoon tomato paste

1 cup chicken stock

3 cups chopped cooked chicken or a whole cooked chicken, cut in eighths

Salt

Freshly ground black pepper

5 tablespoons minced parsley

½ cup bread crumbs

Many homemakers cook chicken soup for Shabbat, a delicious and appropriately festive dish for the start of the meal. The question then is what to do with the chicken that gave its all for the soup? This dish is perfect — far more important than most leftover dishes. If you don't have cooked chicken meat, you can start from scratch with chicken pieces.

1. Sauté the shallot and garlic in a skillet in 3 tablespoons of the olive or vegetable oil until the shallot softens, 5 to 8 minutes.

2. Pour in the wine vinegar and raise the heat. Stirring, boil until almost all the vinegar evaporates. Add the tomato, tomato paste, and chicken stock. Simmer for 15 to 20 minutes.

3. Put the chicken pieces in the sauce. Season with salt and pepper. Cook just long enough to heat the chicken. You can serve the chicken immediately, sprinkled with parsley, but the dish is better with a gratinéed parsley and bread-crumb crust. Keep the sauce at a very gentle simmer and preheat the broiler. Combine the bread crumbs and parsley with the remaining 1 tablespoon of olive oil. It will be fairly dry. Transfer the contents of the skillet to a 5- to 6-cup gratin dish; sprinkle it with the bread-crumb mixture. Place the dish under the broiler for a few minutes, until the parsley–bread-crumb mixture starts to brown. Serve immediately.

AHEAD OF TIME NOTE:

The dish can be made in advance up to the final browning under the broiler. Reheat it gently before completing the dish.

ROCK CORNISH GAME HENS STUFFED WITH BULGAR

6 1- to 1¼-pound game hens

3 cups Bulgar Stuffing (see page 112)

6 tablespoons vegetable oil

It's unclear when crossbreeding the Cornish and white Plymouth Rock breeds yielded the handy bantamweight Rock Cornish game hen. They are practically all breast and are very tender.

1. Preheat the oven to 500 degrees (see Note).

2. Wash and dry the hens.

3. Stuff each hen with ½ cup of the stuffing. Skewer the openings closed, threading the skewers through the loose skin.

4. Rub each hen with about 1 tablespoon of the oil. As each is rubbed, place it on a rack in a roasting pan. Place the pan in the oven and roast the hens for 30 to 35 minutes. Remove the skewers and serve one hen to each diner.

NOTE:

I've become a fan of Barbara Kafka's high-temperature method of roasting. It can, however, fill your kitchen and other parts of the house with smoke; you may even have to disengage the smoke detector. If this is more trouble than you care to go to, roast the birds at 375 degrees for 45 minutes.

BULGAR STUFFING

1 cup bulgar

2 cups chicken stock or
water, boiling

¼ cup toasted pine nuts or
chopped walnuts (see
Note)

2 tablespoons lemon juice

¼ cup chopped parsley

¼ cup chopped mint

Salt

Freshly ground black
pepper

This stuffing is delicious and fresh tasting; it suits all poultry.

1. Place the bulgar in a bowl and cover it with the boiling liquid. Soak it for 15 minutes. Drain the bulgar, discarding any liquid left in the bowl.

2. Combine the bulgar with the remaining ingredients, stirring well.

NOTE:

To toast nuts, spread them on a cookie sheet and place in a preheated 350-degree oven. Stir the nuts from time to time; they should give off a nutty smell and their color should deepen in about 10 to 15 minutes. Keep an eye on them; you don't want the nuts to burn.

BRINED TURKEY

Rick Kot, the editor of this book and a friend, has been raving about this method of cooking turkey for some time. And he's not alone. The method was recorded by Jean Anderson in her book *Foods of Portugal* and further popularized by editors at *Cook's Illustrated* magazine. Pam Anderson and Karen Tack wrote about the method in the November/December 1993 issue of *Cook's Illustrated;* with useful sidebars by Jack Bishop, the article is a masterpiece of clarity. Brining the turkey gives the roasted bird a firm texture, with a juicy breast, which may be the secret of kosher turkeys. If you buy a kosher turkey, after brining soak it in fresh water for about 30 minutes, changing the water a few times. The brining takes time, but really no effort. Plan to roast the turkey as soon as possible after it is removed from the brining solution.

Because a stuffing cooked in the bird almost always yields an overcooked turkey (stuffing slows interior cooking), serve this with your favorite stuffing or kugel, cooked separately.

1. Thoroughly rinse the turkey inside and out; reserve the giblets.

2. You need a large pot in which the turkey can fit comfortably — a stock pot is good. Pour the salt into the neck and body cavities; rub salt all over the turkey and into the skin. Put the turkey into the pot and add cold water to cover. Place the turkey in the refrigerator or other cool place for 4 to 6 hours. Remove the turkey from the brine and rinse, inside and out, under cold, running water for 5 to 6 minutes, until salt is no longer visible.

3. Preheat the oven to 400 degrees.

4. Reserving 1 onion, ½ of a carrot, and ½ of a celery stalk, toss half of the remaining onions, carrots, celery, and parsley with 1 tablespoon of the olive oil. Place the vegetable mixture in the cavity of the turkey. Skewer the bird closed to keep the vegetables inside. Truss, or just tie the legs together.

5. Scatter the remaining vegetables on the bottom of a shallow roasting pan; moisten with 1 cup of the stock. Place the

Ingredients

1 12- to 14-pound turkey

2 pounds kosher salt

7 onions, coarsely chopped

6 carrots, coarsely chopped

4 celery stalks, coarsely chopped

6 parsley sprigs

4 tablespoons olive oil

4 cups chicken stock

(continued on next page)

Poultry

turkey on a rack over the vegetables, breast side down. Brush the back of the turkey with some of the remaining olive oil.

6. Roast the turkey for 70 minutes. Remove the pan from the oven. With large wads of paper towels in each hand or several potholders that you are willing to sacrifice, turn the turkey breast-side up. Baste with oil. If your oven is large enough to accommodate the turkey on its side, roast each side for 15 minutes, deducting 15 minutes each from the back and the breast. Add an additional ½ cup of stock if it has all evaporated. Roast for another 45 to 60 minutes, until a thermometer inserted between the leg and the body reads 165 degrees. Transfer the turkey to a cutting board and let it rest for 30 minutes before carving. Remove the vegetables from the cavity and place them on the platter with the carved bird.

7. While the turkey is roasting, start the giblet stock. Put the neck, gizzard, and heart in a saucepan with 4 cups of water and the reserved chopped onion, carrot, and celery. Simmer for the 2 hours the turkey cooks, adding water if necessary to keep the solids covered.

8. To make a gravy, strain the roasting-pan drippings into a large saucepan, pressing down on the solids to get all the flavor and liquid before discarding them. Remove as much fat as you can from the pan juices. Add the pan juices to the giblet stock. If there are brown bits left in the roasting pan, place the roasting pan on the cooktop over medium heat with ½ cup of giblet stock. With a wooden spoon, loosen the bits that have adhered to the pan. When the juices start to simmer, strain the liquid into the saucepan, bring it to boiling, and simmer for a few minutes. You can dice the giblets and add them to the gravy, if you wish. You can also make a roux with the skimmed turkey fat and a little flour. For 3 cups of gravy, heat 4 tablespoons of fat and stir in 5 tablespoons of flour. Cook, stirring, until the roux darkens, about 5 minutes. Add the roux to the liquid. Taste for seasoning. Transfer the gravy to a sauceboat and pass it with the turkey.

NOTE:

This is also a good method for cooking chicken. For a 3½- to 4-pound chicken use ⅔ to 1 cup of salt. Set the chicken in the brine for 3 hours. Use 2 onions, 2 carrots, 1 celery stalk, and 3 parsley sprigs. You need turn the chicken only once and roast it for 1 hour.

BROILED ORANGE DUCK

Serves 6 to 8

Duck is a welcome change from chicken. Though there are lots of techniques for dealing with the fat, none is as easy as this method. This simple and delicious recipe is one I learned decades ago from *Michael Field's Cooking School*.

1. Trim the quarterd ducks of excess fat and remove the wing tips. Wash the pieces and dry them with paper towels.

2. Combine the juices, ginger, onion, garlic, and bay leaves in a bowl or pot large enough to hold the duck pieces. Add the duck and spoon the marinade over all the pieces. Marinate in the refrigerator for 3 to 24 hours, turning occasionally.

3. Just before cooking the duck, make the sauce. With a swivel-bladed vegetable peeler, remove the peel from the oranges. Slice it into julienne strips. Turn one orange at a time on its side and slice off the top and bottom. Stand the orange on one of the flat sides and, following the curve of the fruit, remove the white pith that remains. Slice the oranges thinly across the segments; work over a bowl to catch the juice, which you should add to the sauce in the next step. Set the orange slices aside.

4. In a saucepan, combine the sugar and wine vinegar. Cook for 3 to 4 minutes, until the sugar dissolves and the mixture starts to boil. Pour the chicken stock into the saucepan. Add the orange peel and juice.

5. Remove the duck from its marinade. Strain the marinade into the simmering sauce. Simmer for 15 to 20 minutes, until the sauce reduces slightly.

6. Preheat the broiler. Set the rack about 4 inches from the heat source.

2 or 3 ducks (about 4 to 5 pounds each), quartered
1 cup orange juice
1 cup lemon juice
1 tablespoon grated fresh ginger
2 cups sliced onion
2 tablespoons sliced garlic
4 bay leaves, crumbled

SAUCE:

5 navel oranges
1 tablespoon sugar
2 tablespoons red-wine vinegar
1 cup chicken stock

Watercress or parsley, for garnish

(continued on next page)

7. Prick the duck pieces all over with a skewer or the tines of a fork — this will help to release the fat. Lay the duck pieces on a broiler rack, skin side down. Broil for 30 minutes. Turn the pieces and broil them skin side up for 15 minutes. During the last 5 minutes, move the rack as close to the element as possible without igniting the duck. You want crisp skin, not burned, and the duck should be cooked, not rare.

8. When the duck is done, put it on a heated platter. Garnish the platter with the reserved orange slices and watercress or parsley. Pass the sauce separately.

DUCK WITH POMEGRANATE AND WALNUT SAUCE

The he ancient Persians so esteemed the walnut tree that they reserved the nuts for the king. The pomegranate, too, probably originated in Persia, and it is significant in Jewish literature and lore: its seeds are said to represent the 613 mitzvoth in the Torah, and the fruit is mentioned in the Song of Songs. The Jewish population of Iran carried this dish with them to London and Los Angeles, two cities with a large Iranian Jewish population. It is often made with duck, which maintains its flavor and texture against the assertive sauce. But it's also good with chicken. For a real feast, the dish is sometimes garnished with tiny meatballs. It's usually served with rice.

1 5- to 6-pound duck, cut into 6 to 8 pieces

2 tablespoons vegetable oil

½ pound (2 cups) shelled walnuts

2 cups chopped onion

2 cups duck or chicken stock

Salt

Freshly ground black pepper

MEATBALLS:

½ pound ground lamb, veal, or beef

½ cup minced onion

Salt

Freshly ground black pepper

1 tablespoon vegetable oil

4 tablespoons pomegranate molasses

2 tablespoons sugar

1. Wash and dry the duck pieces. Remove excess fat and the skin to which it is attached and save it for rendering (see page 36). With a skewer or the tines of a fork, puncture the duck pieces all over — this will release more fat, which can then be discarded after the next step.

2. Heat 2 tablespoons of vegetable oil in a large skillet. Sauté the duck pieces until they are lightly colored. Remove the duck to a platter and pour the fat into a can or large bowl.

3. Pulse the walnuts in a food processor for a few minutes. They should retain some texture; don't make a puree.

4. Return 2 tablespoons of the duck fat to the skillet and fry the walnuts over very low heat just until they begin to change color. Be careful, because they burn quickly. Scrape the walnuts into a bowl with a rubber spatula. Add 2 more tablespoons of duck fat to the skillet.

5. Add the chopped onion and sauté until soft and lightly colored. Return the duck to the skillet and add the stock, which should cover the bottom of the pan by about 1 inch. Add salt and pepper. Bring the stock to simmering, cover the skillet, and cook slowly for 20 minutes.

(continued on next page)

6. Add the walnuts and cook for an additional 20 minutes.

7. Remove the duck to a platter and strain the sauce into a bowl. If you have time, refrigerate the sauce so you can easily remove the additional fat that will harden on the top. If you don't have the time, spoon off the fat that rises to the top of the bowl.

8. If you want to make the meatballs, combine the lamb, veal, or beef and the onion; season with salt and pepper. With moistened hands, make meatballs the size of marbles; you will have about 20. Heat the vegetable oil in a large skillet and fry the meatballs until they are brown on all sides. Reserve.

9. Return the defatted sauce to the skillet. Add the pomegranate molasses and the sugar, stirring well to dissolve the molasses. Add the duck pieces and bring to simmering. Taste for seasoning. Reheat the meatballs in the skillet in which they were made if they have been waiting.

10. Transfer the duck pieces to a heated platter and surround them with the meatballs. Pass the sauce in a gravy boat.

ROAST GOOSE

Roast goose is a cause for celebration not only for the succulence of its flesh but for the joy of having the fat and the stock that can be made from the carcass. This twice-cooked method makes preparation easy on the cook. I learned about it from an article in *The Los Angeles Times* by Michele Hunevan.

1. Preheat the oven to 350 degrees.

2. Remove the deposits of fat from the cavity of the goose, along with some neck skin (see page 120 for instructions on rendering); wash and dry the bird inside and out. Prick the skin (but not too deeply — try not to penetrate the flesh).

3. Make a paste of the garlic and salt by pressing the garlic through a press and combining it with the salt. Rub it all over the bird.

4. Pierce the lemons with a thin skewer, halve the onion, and quarter the apples. Put them in the cavity of the goose.

5. Put the goose on a rack in a large heavy roasting pan. Place the giblets and neck (but not the liver) and 2 cups of water in the pan. Roast the goose for 1½ to 2 hours, or until a thermometer inserted between the thigh and the body registers 145 degrees. After 1 hour of cooking, remove most of the liquid from the bottom of the pan with a bulb baster. Hold a large measuring cup or other heat-resistant vessel close to the roasting pan — you don't want the hot fat traveling too far. After the goose reaches an internal temperature of 145 degrees, remove it from the oven and let it sit for at least 30 minutes or up to several hours.

6. Raise the oven temperature to 450 degrees about 1 hour before you plan to serve. Cook the goose for 30 to 40 minutes, until the skin is brown and crisp and the internal temperature reaches 165 degrees. Let the goose rest 20 to 30 minutes before carving to serve.

7. While the goose rests, remove the rest of the fat from the pan and add it to the measuring cup. By this time the fat will have risen to the top and the cooking juice will be on the bottom. Gently pour off the fat into another container

1 12-pound goose, defrosted (see Note, page 120)

8 garlic cloves, peeled

2 tablespoons kosher salt

3 lemons

1 large onion

2 tart apples

1 cup cooking juice, poultry stock, or water

(continued on next page)

(see below for what to do with this fat). Make a thin gravy with the remaining pan juice, or add other liquid to the pan. Bring the liquid to boiling and scrape up the brown bits on the bottom of the pan. Add any juice that has accumulated around the resting goose. Serve the gravy in a sauceboat to accompany the goose.

NOTE:

Most geese in this country are sold frozen. Leave to defrost in your refrigerator for 48 to 72 hours.

GOOSE FAT

Liquid goose fat from roasting pan

Solid goose fat taken from the raw bird

Neck skin

3 to 4 tablespoons water

It turns out that fat that's liquid at room temperature (chicken fat, goose fat, even lard, though that's irrelevant here) may not be as good for you as a workout, but it's better for you than hydrologized fat (margarine). This benefit from cooking a goose would almost be worth the trouble even without the delicious flesh of the bird.

1. Place the liquid goose fat in a heavy saucepan.

2. Cut the solid fat and skin into small pieces and add them to the saucepan along with the water. Bring the fat to boiling and simmer it gently for about 1 hour. Strain the rendered fat through several thicknesses of clean cheesecloth or through a coffee filter. Transfer it to a plastic container and store it in the freezer until needed. It will keep for months if frozen.

GOOSE STOCK

Goose carcass

Water

Here's another benefit to roasting a goose. It won't be as rich as a poultry stock made from a whole, uncooked bird, but it's useful to have around.

When you're satisfied that no more meat remains for picking, put the carcass, in pieces, in a heavy stockpot. Add water to cover, bring to boiling, lower the heat, partially cover the pot, and cook the carcass for 2 to 3 hours. The bones will resemble a Georgia O'Keeffe desert painting. Strain the stock into a large bowl and let it cool, then refrigerate it to harden any fat. Remove the fat and store the stock in small batches in the freezer.

MEAT

*He who labors
before the Sabbath
shall feast upon the Sabbath.*

HEBREW PROVERB

MEAT HAS ALWAYS MEANT A celebration or a holiday, because it has always been expensive. Historically, it's been reserved for Shabbat and special occasions. Kashrut requires that meat be koshered not later than seventy-two hours after slaughtering. This leaves little time for the meat to tenderize, which is why Jews have always preferred long, slow cooking for their meat dishes.

The recipes in this chapter include those for beef and lamb, in stews, pot roasts, minced dishes. Some are eastern European, some are Sephardic, all are Shabbat worthy and easily made in advance.

BARBECUED BRISKET

Here's a classic American dish that uses a kosher cut of meat. Its long, slow oven cooking (four to five hours) is a boon for the busy Shabbat cook. This spice rub is hot; use less cayenne if you prefer milder food.

1. Combine all the ingredients except the brisket in a small bowl. Mix well.

2. Rub the spice mixture into the brisket and let it sit for an hour or two in a roasting pan.

3. Preheat the oven to 300 degrees.

4. Cook the brisket in the oven for 1 hour; turn and cook for another hour. Cover the brisket with foil or a lid and let it cook undisturbed for 2½ to 3 hours more. Remove the brisket from the oven and let it sit for 15 minutes before slicing.

2 tablespoons toasted cumin seeds, ground (see Note)

3 or 4 large garlic cloves, peeled and mashed

1 tablespoon dry mustard

2 teaspoons paprika

1 tablespoon cayenne (or less, to taste)

1 teaspoon salt

1 tablespoon freshly ground black pepper

½ cup dark brown sugar

4 pounds brisket (see Note, page 125)

NOTE:

Toast cumin seeds in a dry cast-iron skillet over medium heat. Toss continuously for about 5 minutes, watching carefully; they turn from toasted to burned quickly. Grind the seeds in a mortar with a pestle or in an electric grinder.

AHEAD OF TIME NOTE:

This can be made in advance and reheated.

Meat

BRISKET IN RED WINE

1 5-pound brisket (see Note)

2 large onions, peeled and halved

3 large garlic cloves, peeled and halved

1 teaspoon paprika

1 teaspoon coarse salt

1 teaspoon freshly ground black pepper

6 carrots, scraped

1 cup dry red wine

Brisket remains a Shabbat favorite: it feeds a lot of people without much extra effort. It's also a nostalgic choice among Ashkenazim, because beef was expensive and uncommon in eastern Europe and was therefore special enough to serve on Shabbat. This recipe is another from Gale Robinson, a childhood friend and a creative cook with a remarkable taste memory. Like all pot roasts, this benefits from being made a day ahead.

1. Preheat the oven to 500 degrees.

2. Place the brisket in the bottom of a roasting pan or shallow ovenproof dish that will comfortably hold the meat and vegetables.

3. Rub the brisket with the cut sides of the onions. Repeat with the garlic. Then cut the onions into eighths.

4. Combine the paprika, salt, and pepper in a small bowl. Rub the mixture into the brisket.

5. Roast the brisket in the very hot oven for 20 minutes, until the top is brown. Remove the brisket from the oven and reduce the heat to 350 degrees.

6. Scatter the onions and garlic and whole carrots around the meat. Pour the wine over the vegetables. Cover the roaster loosely with foil and roast for 2 to 3 hours, until the meat is very tender. Remove the meat from the vegetables and liquid. When the meat cools, wrap and refrigerate it. Set the carrots aside. Refrigerate the liquid and onions until the fat hardens on the surface. Discard the fat.

7. Puree the onions, liquid, and 2 of the roasted carrots in a food processor.

8. Slice the brisket thinly, against the grain.

9. Coat the bottom of an ovenproof serving dish with a little of the gravy. Add the brisket slices, spread them with a little more gravy, and reheat the meat in a 350 degree oven for 20 to 30 minutes, until the brisket is hot. Heat the remaining gravy in a saucepan and pass it in a sauceboat with the brisket.

NOTE:

I always prefer a whole brisket. Though it's got more fat than the first cut, the fat gives it more flavor. It's becoming more and more difficult to find whole briskets, however. If you do find one, it will be larger than 5 pounds, but will shrink considerably. Trim it of excess fat; enough will remain to intensify the meat's flavor.

BRAISED
SHORT RIBS

6 pounds short ribs, cut into 3-inch lengths

5 tablespoons vegetable oil

¼ cup flour

2 tablespoons toasted cumin seeds, ground (see Note, page 123)

2 teaspoons salt

1 teaspoon freshly ground pepper

2 cups minced onion

2 cups minced carrot

2 tablespoons chopped garlic

½ teaspoon allspice

2 cups beef stock, fresh, canned, or cube

4 tablespoons chopped parsley

Short ribs and flanken are both cut from the ribs that extend from the back of the cow toward the belly and are found in the plate section as well as the rib, chuck, and brisket section. Short ribs are cut parallel to the rib bone and between the ribs; flanken are cut across the rib bones. They are both delicious. Tough and fatty, they are full of flavor. The braising makes them tender and the initial searing burns off much of the fat.

These are best made a day in advance to allow the fat to harden on top of the sauce. Serve with Mamaliga (page 173), boiled potatoes, steamed noodles, or Potato and Parsnip Kugel (page 182).

1. Dry the short ribs with paper towels.

2. Heat 3 tablespoons of the oil in a large, heavy Dutch oven or skillet.

3. On a plate, combine with a fork the flour, 1 tablespoon of the cumin, the salt, and the pepper. Dredge the short ribs in the flour mixture, shaking the excess off over the sink. Brown the ribs, in batches, in the hot oil. Don't crowd the pan or the ribs won't brown. Remove each rib to a platter when it is done. When all the meat is browned, pour out the accumulated fat.

4. Heat the remaining oil in the skillet. Add the onion, carrot, and garlic to the pan. Stir over low heat for 15 minutes or so, until the onion is very soft and barely colored. Stir in the remaining cumin and the allspice. Return the ribs to the pot, add the stock, bring it to simmering, cover, and cook over low heat until the meat is tender when pierced with a fork. It will take anywhere from 1 to 2 hours, depending on the meat.

5. Strain the juice into a wide bowl. If you have time, refrigerate it to allow the fat to harden on the top for easy removal. If you don't have time, remove as much fat as you can with a wide, flat spoon. Reheat the ribs and sauce slowly and serve sprinkled with parsley, accompanied by one of the suggestions above.

NEW ENGLAND BOILED DINNER

This one-dish meal is perfect for Shabbat: it can be made a day or a few hours in advance, though there is no last-minute work to distract the cook from other preparations. New Englanders have been making this for generations with corned beef. It can also be made with brisket. But I love it with flanken — a nice Jewish cut.

1. Put the flanken in a pot large enough to hold it and all the remaining ingredients in one layer. Cover it with 4 to 6 cups of cold water. Bring the water to boiling and simmer for 15 minutes, skimming the foam that rises.

2. Add the onions, garlic, celery, salt, and bouquet garni. Partially cover the pot and cook gently for about 1½ hours.

3. Add the carrots, leeks, and turnips; simmer for 40 minutes.

4. While the meat and vegetables are simmering, cook the potatoes and cabbage. Though you can cook these in the larger pot with the meat, I think they taste better, fresher, when cooked separately. Put the potatoes in a saucepan with water to cover. Bring to boiling and simmer for 15 minutes; timing depends on the size of the potatoes.

5. Quarter and core the cabbage, then slice it in eighths. Place it in a steamer over an inch or so of water. Cover the cabbage with the wilted outer leaves that you would otherwise discard. Steam for 10 to 15 minutes.

6. Serve the meat, vegetables, and potatoes on a large platter, moistened with a little broth and accompanied with mustard, pickles, and roasted beets.

Ingredients

- 6 pounds flanken (in 8 to 10 pieces)
- 2 onions, quartered
- 4 garlic cloves, peeled but left whole
- 2 celery stalks, cut into chunks
- 2 tablespoons salt
- Bouquet garni of 3 parsley sprigs, celery leaves (from the ribs), 2 teaspoons whole black peppercorns, 2 bay leaves, tied in washed cheesecloth
- 6 carrots, cut into chunks
- 6 leeks, trimmed and well washed
- 4 white turnips, peeled and quartered
- 8 to 10 small red potatoes
- 1 small head cabbage
- Mustard
- Pickles
- Roasted beets (see Note)

NOTE:

To roast beets, leave the tail and about ½ inch of stem on them. Wash them carefully, taking care not to pierce them. Place the beets in a shallow pan with a little water; cover. Roast them in a preheated 400-degree oven until tender, 1 to 2 hours depending on the age and size of the beets. When cool enough to handle, slice off the stem and tail and slip the beets out of their skins.

Meat

WINTER BEEF STEW

3 tablespoons olive or vegetable oil

3 pounds boneless chuck, cut into 2-inch cubes

5 leeks, washed carefully and chopped, including some green top (about 5 cups)

3 tablespoons flour

½ cup red-wine vinegar

2 cups beef broth, fresh, canned, or diluted cube (see Note)

2 bay leaves

Salt

Freshly ground pepper

¼ cup minced parsley

The leeks and long cooking of the tasty but not-so-tender cut of meat makes this an ideal winter Shabbat dish; the vinegar adds an unexpected piquancy. The dish benefits from being made a day ahead. Serve with noodles or steamed potatoes or Mamaliga (page 173).

1. Heat the oil in a heavy casserole dish or Dutch oven. Dry the meat with paper towels and brown it, in batches so as not to crowd the pan, until it's nicely colored. Remove each batch to a platter as it is done.

2. In the same pan, sauté the leeks until soft, about 10 minutes. Add the flour and cook, stirring, for a few minutes, until it is thoroughly mixed with the leeks.

3. Add the wine vinegar, raise the heat, and scrape up all the brown bits in the bottom of the pot. Almost all the vinegar will evaporate. Lower the heat, return the beef to the pot, add the broth, bay leaves, salt, and pepper. Cover the pot and simmer until the meat is very tender. You can also cook the stew in a 325-degree oven. Depending on the cut and quality of the meat, the stew should take about 2 hours. Cool, cover, and refrigerate it if not serving immediately.

4. Reheat the stew slowly and serve it sprinkled with parsley.

NOTE:

Through the years I've learned from cookbook writers, those who work abroad particularly, the benefits of a good-quality bouillon cube. There are several brands on the market that are excellent, and I urge you to use them, sometimes heavily diluted, when there's no stock in the freezer.

POT ROAST
BRAISED IN
VINEGAR

Though brisket is a popular choice for pot roast, don't overlook other available cuts; this slow-cooked chuck roast, for example, is delicious. Chuck is not a lean cut, which is why it is so flavorful.

4 tablespoons olive oil
2 cups minced onion
1 cup minced celery
1 cup minced carrot
1 boneless chuck roast,
  4 to 5 pounds
1 tablespoon vegetable oil
½ cup red-wine vinegar
  Salt
  Freshly ground black
  pepper
2 cups beef stock

1. Heat the olive oil in a deep casserole dish. Add the onion, celery, and carrot. Cook slowly, stirring, for about 15 minutes, until the vegetables are soft.

2. Dry the meat well. Heat the vegetable oil in a large skillet. Sear the meat on all sides over medium-high heat. This will take about 15 minutes. Transfer the meat to the vegetables.

3. Pour the wine vinegar into the skillet; bring it to a rapid boil and deglaze the pan. Pour the liquid over the meat and season it with salt and pepper.

4. Add the beef stock to the casserole dish, bring to boiling, cover the dish, and cook over very low heat for 2 to 3 hours, until the meat is quite tender; test after 2 hours. Alternatively, you can cook the meat in a 350-degree oven.

5. When the meat is done, remove it to a board and slice it across the grain into ½-inch-thick slices. Slice off excess fat.

6. Strain the liquid, skimming as much fat as you can from the surface. Puree the liquid and the vegetables. Transfer the pureed liquid to a clean saucepan and bring it to boiling. Boil the liquid down rapidly to intensify the flavor and create a somewhat thick sauce. Taste for seasoning. Add the sliced meat and reheat at a gentle simmer.

NOTE:

If you want to make the pot roast in advance (and it benefits from advance cooking), cook through step 5, leaving the meat unsliced. Store the meat, liquid, and vegetables separately in the refrigerator. Before serving, remove the hardened fat from the liquid, puree the liquid with the vegetables, slice the meat, and reheat.

Meat

CURRIED MEATBALLS (KOFTA KARI)

1 pound finely ground beef (twice ground through a fine blade)

2 tablespoons bread crumbs or matzo meal

1 cup chopped onion

1 large egg, lightly beaten

4 tablespoons chopped parsley

2 tablespoons chopped fresh coriander

2 teaspoons toasted cumin seeds, ground (see Note, page 123)

1 teaspoon ground turmeric

Salt

Freshly ground black pepper

FOR FRYING:

Vegetable oil

1 cinnamon stick

3 cardamom pods

6 black peppercorns

4 whole cloves

1 whole dried chili pepper

Meatballs, which originated in the Near East, were spread throughout central Asia by the Persians. Baghdad was a significant center of Jewish learning for twenty-five hundred years. What is today the countries of Iraq and Syria had been a trading area with India, and many Jews emigrated from there to India. Inevitably, Indian foods were adapted to the laws of kashrut and served in Jewish homes. In many Jewish communities meatballs were considered special enough to be served for Shabbat. These certainly are. Serve with boiled rice.

1. With your scrupulously clean hands, combine the meat, bread crumbs or matzo meal, onion, egg, parsley, coriander, cumin, turmeric, salt, and pepper.

2. With moistened hands, shape the mixture into 1- to 1½-inch balls; shape each ball from a heaping tablespoon of meat. You should have 20 to 25 meatballs. As each is made, place it on a platter.

3. For frying, heat ½ inch of oil in a large skillet over medium heat. Add the cinnamon, cardamom, peppercorns, cloves, and chili pepper. Stir. Add the meatballs in one layer — don't crowd the pan. Brown them on all sides — they will cook through later. Remove the meatballs with a slotted spoon and return them to the platter. When all the koftas are brown, set them aside.

4. Strain the oil from the skillet into a bowl. Discard the spices and the chili pepper. Pour 2 tablespoons of the oil back into the skillet.

5. To make the sauce, puree the onion, garlic, and ginger in the processor. Add the puree to the skillet and fry for about 10 minutes, stirring frequently.

6. Combine the cinnamon, coriander, cumin, and chili powder in a small bowl. Add the mixture to the skillet and sauté for 5 minutes. Add the koftas, 1 cup of cold water (the koftas should be about half submerged), and salt. Bring to simmering, cover, and cook slowly for 30 minutes.

7. To serve, gently spoon the koftas onto a platter and pour the sauce over. Sprinkle with lemon juice.

AHEAD OF TIME NOTE:

You can prepare the koftas through step 4 early in the day you are serving. Or, you can complete the entire dish and reheat it gently at serving time.

SAUCE:

1 cup chopped onion

4 garlic cloves, peeled

2 tablespoons chopped fresh ginger

2 teaspoons ground cinnamon

2 teaspoons ground coriander seed

2 teaspoons toasted cumin seeds, ground

1 teaspoon chili powder

Salt

2 teaspoons lemon juice

MEATBALLS
WITH PIPERADE

MEATBALLS:

- 2 pounds ground beef
- 1 cup minced onion
- ½ cup matzo meal or bread crumbs
- 2 eggs, lightly beaten
- 4 tablespoons minced parsley
- 2 tablespoons minced garlic
- Salt
- Freshly ground black pepper
- 4 tablespoons vegetable or olive oil

SAUCE:

- 4 red, green, or yellow peppers, or a combination
- 4 tablespoons olive oil
- 1 cup thinly sliced onion
- 3 garlic cloves, peeled and crushed
- 3 cups peeled, chopped tomato, fresh or canned (including some of the juice from canned tomato)
- Pinch cayenne
- Pinch sugar

Ground meat was popular among Jews because grinding helped tenderize the usually tough kosher cuts of beef and was also a good way to stretch expensive beef. Dressed up with a pepper sauce, this is an appropriate New World Shabbat meal. Serve with rice or boiled potatoes.

1. Combine all the meatball ingredients, except the oil, in a large bowl. Mix thoroughly with your hands.

2. Moisten your hands and form the mixture into ovals or balls. Use about 1 rounded tablespoonful for each meatball. You should have 45 to 50 meatballs. Set the meatballs aside on a platter until all are made.

3. Heat the oil in a large skillet. Fry the meatballs, in a single layer, until brown on all sides. As they are done, remove them and set them aside. Repeat until all the meatballs are fried. (They don't complete their cooking at this stage.) Wipe out the skillet with paper toweling.

4. To make the sauce, wash, core, peel (see Note), and cut the peppers into julienne strips. Heat the oil in the skillet and add the peppers with the remaining sauce ingredients. Sauté, stirring for 5 or 6 minutes. Add the meatballs and cook over low heat for 30 minutes. Serve immediately.

NOTE:

Marcella Hazan has a simple and clever technique for peeling peppers: remove the skin with a vegetable peeler. It's quick and easy. If a little skin remains on the pepper, as it will in the creases, it doesn't matter.

AHEAD OF TIME NOTE:

You can cook the dish through step 3 several hours in advance of serving.

BEEF SHEPHERD'S PIE

I love shepherd's pie and thought a kosher version would be an excellent Shabbat dish. Traditional shepherd's pie is made with lamb, and the potato topping is usually mashed with butter and milk. This kosher version is festive and delicious.

1. Boil the potatoes until tender. Peel and mash them with 2 tablespoons of the olive oil and enough meat stock to moisten them into a spreadable mass.

2. In a large heavy skillet, sauté the onion in the remaining 2 tablespoons of olive oil until very soft, about 15 minutes.

3. Add the garlic and beef. Stir, breaking up the lumps with a wooden utensil, until the beef is no longer pink. Add the tomato, bay leaf, thyme, salt, and pepper. Cover the pan and cook for 20 minutes.

4. Add the parsley to the meat.

5. Preheat the broiler.

6. Pour off the accumulated liquid and fat from the meat. Spread the meat in a 2-quart gratin dish. Smooth the potatoes over the meat or pipe them on through a pastry bag. Sprinkle with a little olive oil. Broil for about 5 minutes, until the top is brown.

AHEAD OF TIME NOTE:
If you make the dish in advance, reheat it on top of the stove before you brown the potato topping under the broiler.

1½ pounds all-purpose potatoes

4 tablespoons olive oil

½ to 1 cup meat stock

1 cup minced onion

2 tablespoons minced garlic

1½ pounds ground beef

1 cup chopped tomato (fresh or canned)

Bay leaf

½ teaspoon dried thyme

Salt

Freshly ground black pepper

6 tablespoons minced parsley

Meat

3 tablespoons vegetable oil

2 cups coarsely chopped onion

½ cup packed brown sugar

35 ounces canned peeled tomato, packed in tomato juice

2 cups tomato sauce

1 2- to 2½-pound green cabbage

1 onion, peeled

2 pounds ground beef

2 eggs, lightly beaten

¼ cup uncooked white rice

2 tablespoons ketchup

Salt

Freshly ground black pepper

½ pound pitted prunes (about 1½ cups)

½ cup raisins

Grated peel and juice of 1 lemon

STUFFED CABBAGE

Stuffed cabbage was one of my mother's specialties, and it was a happy Shabbos, indeed, when we were treated to this dish. She always served it as a first course, but with chicken soup as a starter, and perhaps a fish course, too, it makes a wonderful main course.

Stuffed cabbage is one of the many dishes that benefited from the plenty of the New World. In Lomzha — then Russia, now Poland — where my grandmother made her stuffed cabbage, tomatoes were surely a luxury item and rice was probably unknown. Yet this dish has become one of the signatures of Ashkenazic cooking.

1. Heat the oil in a Dutch oven. Sauté the onion over medium heat until soft, about 15 minutes.

2. Add the brown sugar, mashing out any lumps against the pot with a wooden spoon. Working over the pot, break up the tomato with your fingers and add it along with the juice and the tomato sauce. Cover the pot and simmer the sauce for about 1 hour.

3. While the sauce cooks, prepare the cabbage. Cut out and discard the core. Submerge the cabbage in a large pot of boiling water; cover and, off heat, let sit for 15 minutes.

4. For the filling, grate the onion directly into the meat in a bowl. Add the eggs, rice, ketchup, salt, and pepper. Mix gently with your hands. If the mixture seems dense and heavy, add up to ½ cup of warm water.

5. Remove the cabbage from the hot water. Carefully peel off the leaves, one by one, without tearing them. If any leaves remain stiff, put them back into the water and bring to boiling. Remove the leaves as soon as they are limp, 2 to 3 minutes. The leaves must be pliable enough to fold without tearing but stiff enough to hold the filling. Shave off the hard ribs with a small, sharp knife. Shred the center leaves, too small to be stuffed, and add them to the sauce. Cut the large outer leaves in half.

6. Place about ⅓ cup of the meat mixture into the center of each cabbage leaf. Fold the leaves to completely enclose the filling. As each is done, place it in the sauce. Form any left-over meat into meatballs and add them to the pot. Finally, add the prunes, raisins, lemon peel, and lemon juice. Cook slowly, covered, for about 1½ hours.

AHEAD OF TIME NOTE:
The stuffed cabbage can be refrigerated, after cooling, for several days; it also freezes well for several months.

STUFFED BREAST OF VEAL

1 veal breast, 8 to 10
   pounds trimmed weight

2 thick slices stale bread,
   crusts trimmed

½ skinless, boneless chicken
   breast (½ pound)

½ pound ground beef

1 egg, lightly beaten

¼ cup chopped walnuts

1 teaspoon rosemary

   Nutmeg

   Salt

   Freshly ground black
   pepper

1 tablespoon olive oil

Edda Servi Machlin, chronicler of Italian-Jewish food, specu-lates that this recipe was an attempt by the Jews of her home-town, Pitigliano, to create a dish that rivaled the slices of roasted piglet sold in the town square during a fall festival. This is my adaptation of the dish. Following is an Ashkenazic stuffing.

Breast of veal doesn't offer a lot of meat in relation to its weight and size. But it's a natural for stuffing and satisfying to eat.

1. Ask the butcher to cut a pocket in the veal breast and to crack the breastbone between the ribs to simplify slicing.

2. Preheat the oven to 400 degrees.

3. Soak the bread briefly in warm water to just cover. Squeeze out the moisture and put the bread in a mixing bowl.

4. Coarsely chop the chicken and grind it in a food processor until it is the same consistency as the beef. Add the chicken to the mixing bowl along with the beef, egg, nuts, rose-mary, a grating of nutmeg, salt, and pepper. You'll have about 3 cups of stuffing.

5. Rub the veal breast inside and out with salt and pepper. Loosely fill the pocket of the veal breast with stuffing. (If you have any left over, place it in the oven for the last hour of cooking.) Brush the outside of the breast with oil. Place the breast on a rack in a roasting pan, rib side down. Roast it for 30 minutes; reduce the heat to 350 degrees and roast for an additional 2 to 2½ hours, until the breast is brown and crisp. Remove it from the oven and let it rest for 15 min-utes. To serve, remove the stuffing to a serving bowl and slice the veal between the ribs.

ASHKENAZIC STUFFING
FOR BREAST OF VEAL

Follow the directions for cooking the veal breast above.

1. In a large skillet, sauté the onion in 2 tablespoons of the oil over gentle heat for 15 minutes or so — it should be very soft but not colored. Add the celery and carrot and sauté for an additional 10 minutes. Remove the vegetables with a slotted spoon to a large bowl.

2. Add the mushrooms to the skillet along with the remaining oil. Sauté them until they give up their liquid. Combine them with the other vegetables.

3. Moisten the bread under running water. Squeeze the water out with your hands. Beat the bread into the vegetables with a wooden spoon, along with the eggs, shmaltz or oil, salt and pepper to taste, and parsley. You'll have 4 to 4½ cups of stuffing.

4. Stuff the veal pocket with the mixture. Put any leftover stuffing in an ovenproof dish; place it in the oven with the veal during the last hour of roasting, basting it with the pan juices from time to time. When serving, combine in a serving bowl the stuffing from the veal with the stuffing cooked separately.

2 cups chopped onion

3 tablespoons olive or vegetable oil

1 cup chopped celery

1 cup chopped carrot

4 cups sliced mushrooms

5 cups cubed day-old French bread, crusts removed

2 eggs, lightly beaten

2 tablespoons shmaltz (page 36) or olive oil

Salt

Freshly ground black pepper

½ cup chopped parsley

NOTE:
This is good as a kugel, without the veal.

SHABBAT COUSCOUS

1 cup dried chickpeas

1 teaspoon toasted cumin seeds, crushed (see Note, page 123)

½ teaspoon cinnamon

1 teaspoon ground ginger

¼ teaspoon ground cloves

½ teaspoon turmeric

½ teaspoon ground coriander seed

1 garlic clove, peeled

3 medium onions

2 tablespoons olive oil

4 pounds first-cut brisket

1 3½-pound chicken

5 or 6 parsley sprigs

¼ teaspoon saffron threads, crushed

Salt

Freshly ground black pepper

5 or 6 carrots, cut into large chunks

1½ to 2 pounds zucchini (about 4 medium)

¾ to 1 pound yellow summer squash

4 cups quick-cooking couscous (yields 12 cups cooked)

½ cup raisins

FOR SERVING:

Moroccan Salads (page 222)

Harissa (page 140)

I did some cooking with my friend Arthur Schwartz, a New York broadcaster, journalist, and cookbook author. Couscous was on the agenda. By fabulous coincidence, as we were about to develop a recipe, his friend Esther McManus called. Mrs. McManus is Moroccan (though Mr. McManus is not) and a consultant to Le Bus, a restaurant and wholesale bakery in Philadelphia. She shared this recipe with us.

1. Soak the chickpeas overnight in water to cover.

2. In a blender or a food processor, make a paste with the cumin, cinnamon, ginger, cloves, turmeric, coriander, garlic, 1 of the onions, and the olive oil. Spread the paste over the brisket and the chicken and let them sit a minimum of 20 minutes, or overnight in the refrigerator if you have the time.

3. In a heavy pot large enough to ultimately accommodate all the ingredients, sweat the brisket over low heat for a few minutes. This will color the brisket and give added flavor to the broth. Add the remaining 2 onions and the parsley, cover the meat with cold water, about 4 quarts, and bring to simmering. Remove a little simmering water to a small saucepan and add the saffron. Simmer for 10 minutes and return the saffron liquid to the pot. Add salt and pepper. Simmer the meat, partially covered, for 1½ hours, skimming the foam as it rises.

4. Put the chickpeas into a saucepan with water to cover. Bring the water to boiling and cook the chickpeas until tender — anywhere from 30 minutes to 2 hours, depending on their age. When they are done, set them aside in their liquid.

5. After the meat has cooked for 1½ hours, add the chicken. Simmer the chicken gently with the brisket for 45 minutes to an hour, until tender when pierced with a fork. Remove the chicken when it's done.

6. About 30 minutes before the meat is done, add the carrots to the pot. About 15 minutes before the end of cooking, remove 3 cups of broth from the stockpot and put it in a

medium-size sauté pan or stove-top casserole — it's for cooking the zucchini and yellow squash.

7. Quarter the zucchini and yellow squash and cook them gently in the simmering broth, covered, for about to 15 minutes, until just tender.

8. At the same time, remove 2 more cups of broth. Dilute it with 4 cups of water and bring it to simmering in a saucepan. Add the couscous. Let it boil for a moment or two, then turn off the heat and let it sit, covered, for 5 minutes. Fluff the couscous with a fork, reaching down to the bottom of the pan.

9. Put the cooked squash and its liquid in the large stockpot. Drain and add the chickpeas. Return the chicken to the pot. Let all the elements simmer together for about 10 minutes.

10. At the same time, remove a cup of simmering broth and put the raisins in it to plump.

11. To serve, heap the couscous in a mound on a platter. As you remove it from the pot to the platter, fluff it again with a fork — the bottom will probably be sticky. Slice the brisket and cut the chicken into serving pieces. Arrange the meat on a platter with the squash and chickpeas. Garnish with the raisins. Pour a ladleful of broth over the platter and pass the rest of the broth separately, with a little harissa stirred in, if you like. Serve with the salads and the harissa.

NOTE:

The vegetable selection is flexible — you can use 5 or 6 turnips in addition to or instead of the squash. Winter squash or butternut squash is also good, as is a cheese or pie pumpkin, or calabaza if you shop in a Latino market.

*Yields a rounded ¼ cup,
enough for 8 to 10 servings
of couscous*

HARISSA

½ cup dried red chili
  peppers
2 garlic cloves, peeled
1 tablespoon kosher salt
2 tablespoons coriander
  seeds
1 tablespoon cumin seeds
2 to 4 tablespoons olive oil

This hot condiment accompanies couscous and tagines in Morocco, Tunisia, and Algeria. My friend Arthur Schwartz says mothers make it for their daughters' dowries. If you eat a lot of couscous, you can double or even quadruple the recipe; it keeps forever.

1. Remove the stems from the peppers and shake out the seeds. Be careful — the seeds are hot — use gloves or wash your hands as soon as you finish. Soak the peppers in hot water for 15 to 20 minutes, until they soften.

2. Pound the garlic with half of the salt in a mortar with a pestle until smooth. Remove it to a small bowl. Add the drained peppers to the mortar and pound them to a paste with the remaining salt. Combine the pepper paste with the garlic.

3. Add the coriander and cumin seeds to the mortar; pound until powdered. Return the garlic-and-pepper paste to the mortar and pound, adding olive oil, until the mixture is a smooth paste. Store the harissa in a sealed container in the refrigerator. It will keep indefinitely, or at least until your daughter's wedding.

SWEET AND SOUR TONGUE

A meal that includes tongue is, to my taste, a cause for celebration. This sweet and sour version is particularly popular among Ashkenazim. Tongue is often served as an appetizer.

1. Wash the tongue under cold running water.

2. Bring a large quantity of water to boiling in a Dutch oven along with the onions, garlic, and bay leaves. Add the tongue. Simmer slowly, skimming from time to time, partially covered for 2½ to 3 hours, until the tongue is tender.

3. Let the tongue cool in the broth. As soon as it is cool enough to handle, remove the skin, any bones, and root end. Return it to the broth to cool completely. You can store the tongue in 3 cups of its strained cooking broth in the refrigerator and serve it cold with mustard, or slice the tongue and reheat it for 5 minutes in the hot sweet and sour sauce.

4. To make the sauce, slowly cook the onion in the oil. Stir in the flour and cook for a minute or two. Gradually add the strained tongue broth, stirring until the mixture comes to boiling. Lower the heat, add the lemon juice, honey, and raisins. Simmer for 5 minutes. Makes about 2 cups.

1 4- to 5-pound pickled beef tongue

2 onions, peeled and quartered

3 garlic cloves, peeled and halved

2 bay leaves

SWEET AND SOUR SAUCE:

1 cup chopped onion

3 tablespoons vegetable oil

2 tablespoons flour

2 cups strained tongue broth

3 tablespoons lemon juice

2 tablespoons honey

½ cup raisins

CALF'S TONGUE WITH CAPERS

1 fresh or pickled calf's tongue, about 4 pounds

4 tablespoons oil

6 garlic cloves, peeled and sliced

⅛ teaspoon saffron threads, crushed

Salt

4 tablespoons lemon juice

6 ounces capers, drained

½ cup chopped parsley

Moroccan Jews created a remarkable cuisine. As everywhere, Jews adapted the laws of kashrut to the indigenous ingredients. Worldwide, Jews enjoyed tongue; in North Africa they combine it, as here, with such native plants as capers. The inclusion of saffron indicates it is a holiday dish, for in Morocco, as elsewhere in the Mediterranean, saffron was handpicked and expensive.

1. Wash the tongue and blanch it for 1½ to 2 hours in simmering water. Remove the tongue from the water, and while it is still hot (as hot as you can stand), remove the skin and any bones. This chore is much easier when the tongue is hot. Cut the tongue in thin slices; remove any more bones, though a pickled tongue is not likely to have any. Strain and reserve the liquid in which it cooked.

2. In a large skillet, heat the oil; add the garlic, saffron, and salt. Add the sliced tongue and 2 cups of the liquid in which it cooked. Bring the broth to boiling, lower the heat, partially cover the pan, and simmer for 15 minutes.

3. With a slotted spoon, remove the tongue slices to a platter (or the flat lid that covered the skillet). Raise the heat and reduce the sauce by half.

4. Add the lemon juice, capers, half the parsley, and the tongue. Partially cover again and simmer for another 10 minutes. Serve on a heated platter, sprinkled with the additional parsley.

NOTE:

You can make the tongue in advance, through step 2. You can also finish the cooking and reheat gently just before serving.

CHOUCROUTE GARNI

There has been a Jewish community in Alsace, France, where this dish originates, for hundreds of years. Many Jewish foods have, in fact, been integrated into general Alsatian cuisine. André Soltner, the great chef and former owner of Lutèce restaurant in New York, offers a recipe for Choucroute à la Juive in his book *The Lutèce Cookbook*. Soltner's and the one offered here are made with kosher meats.

Choucroute is French for sauerkraut or pickled cabbage; *garni* means, simply, garnished. Literally, this is a dish of garnished sauerkraut.

1. Preheat the oven to 350 degrees.

2. Wash the sauerkraut in cold water. Squeeze the water out in your hands and pat the sauerkraut dry on paper towels.

3. In a heavy enameled cast-iron pot that has a cover, heat the shmaltz, goose fat, or oil. Slowly cook the onion and carrot, covered, without browning, for a few minutes.

4. Add the sauerkraut, wine, stock or water, and the bouquet garni. Bring to boiling. Cover the sauerkraut with a sheet of greased wax paper, trimmed to fit, and the lid of the pot. Cook in the preheated oven for 1 hour.

5. Bury the corned beef in the sauerkraut and vegetables and cook for another 2 hours.

6. Bring a large pot of water to boiling. Boil the potatoes until done. Remove the potatoes and keep them warm in the pot with the choucroute. Add the knockwurst to the potato water and cook for 10 minutes; add the frankfurters and cook for 15 more minutes.

7. To serve, place the sauerkraut and vegetables on a platter. Slice the corned beef and knockwurst and arrange them on top. Surround the platter with the frankfurters and potatoes. Serve with mustard.

(continued on next page)

4 pounds sauerkraut (see Note)

4 tablespoons shmaltz (page 36), goose fat, or vegetable oil

3 cups sliced onion

2 cups thinly sliced carrot

2 cups dry white wine; Riesling, Traminer, or other Alsatian wine is best

2 cups chicken or beef stock or water

Bouquet garni of 12 juniper berries, crushed, 10 black peppercorns, 2 bay leaves, 2 teaspoons caraway seeds, tied in cheesecloth

3 pounds fresh uncooked corned beef (see Note, page 144)

15 to 18 small new potatoes

1 pound beef knockwurst

¾ pound beef frankfurters Mustard

Meat

143

NOTE:

The best sauerkraut is bought fresh from barrels. If that's un-
available, try the sauerkraut packaged in plastic bags. Your last
choice should be canned sauerkraut.

If your corned beef is precooked, place it on the sauerkraut
only for the last 30 minutes of cooking.

LAMB SHANKS

Lamb shanks are a hearty and easy-to-prepare-in-advance Shabbat dinner. Though in Israel the entire animal is considered kosher, here our rabbis have deemed only the foreshank kosher. The sciatic nerve is the prohibition. Buy your meat from a kosher butcher and you'll have kosher shanks and a wonderful meal. Don't worry about all the garlic — it cooks very slowly in its skin and imparts a soft flavor.

6 meaty lamb shanks (about 6 pounds)

3 tablespoons olive or vegetable oil

4 cups chopped onion

40 to 50 unpeeled garlic cloves, about 4 heads

Salt

Freshly ground black pepper

2 bay leaves

1. Dry the shanks with paper towels. In a heavy pot, with a tight-fitting lid, that will hold them snugly in one layer, brown the shanks in the oil. Scatter the onion and the garlic cloves over the meat; add salt, pepper, bay leaves, and ½ cup water. Cover the pot and cook over low heat for 1½ hours, checking every 20 minutes or so to make sure there is still liquid in the pan. The shanks are done when very tender.

2. Remove the meat to a platter. With a slotted spoon, transfer the onion and garlic to a bowl. Remove the visible fat from the juice in the pan. Boil down the liquid if there's more than a syrupy film in the pan.

3. Squeeze the garlic out of its skin directly into the pot. Mash the garlic into the pan juice. Return the onion to the pan. Put the shanks back in the pan, cover, and reheat if necessary.

AHEAD OF TIME NOTE:

The dish can be cooked completely and reheated, covered, over gentle heat before serving.

Meat

BRAISED LAMB SHOULDER

½ pound dried navy beans

2 tablespoons olive oil

4½ to 5 pounds boned lamb shoulder, tied

2 cups chopped onion

4 garlic cloves, peeled and mashed

2 tablespoons tomato paste

2 tablespoons flour

1 cup chopped carrot

1 cup chopped celery

2 cups chopped leek, including tender green tops

1 tablespoon coarsely ground or crushed black peppercorns

1 tablespoon salt

2 cups dry white wine

4 cups diluted beef broth (see Note)

Several parsley sprigs tied with 2 bay leaves

This dish cooks for 8 hours. All the work is done in advance. The slow cooking of the tough cut of meat creates a flavorful meal that you can eat with a spoon. It's a very satisfying winter dish.

1. Cover the beans with water, bring to boiling, remove from heat, and set aside, covered, while you prepare the rest of the ingredients.

2. Heat the oil in a heavy casserole dish in which all the ingredients will fit. Dry the lamb with paper towels. Brown on all sides, even the ends. Remove to a platter.

3. Add the onion and garlic to the pan and sauté over low heat until soft, about 10 minutes.

4. Preheat the oven to 300 degrees.

5. In a small bowl, combine the tomato paste and flour. Stir this into the casserole dish and cook, stirring, for a few minutes. Add the carrot, celery, and leek. Cook, stirring, for a few minutes. Drain the beans and add them along with the peppercorns and salt. Stir the ingredients to combine, then return the meat to the casserole. Add the wine and stock, bring to simmering, and add the parsley and bay leaves. Cover the casserole and braise the lamb in the oven for 7 to 8 hours.

6. If you have time, remove the meat and strain the liquid into a large bowl. Refrigerate it to allow the fat to harden into a layer on the top, making its removal very easy. If you don't have enough time, remove as much fat as you can with a large spoon. Discard the parsley and bay leaves.

7. To serve, cut the string from the lamb and put the meat on a serving platter. Taste the braising liquid and add salt and pepper if needed. If necessary, reduce it at a hard boil to intensify the flavor. Distribute the beans and vegetables around the meat; moisten it with some of the liquid. Pass the rest in a gravy boat.

If you use a bouillon cube, dilute it with 4 cups of water. If you use fresh stock or broth, dilute 3 cups with 1 cup of water. Don't use canned bouillon; if that's your only choice, use water alone.

AHEAD OF TIME NOTE:
You can make this a few days in advance and reheat it in a 300-degree oven.

LAMB TAGINE

½ teaspoon saffron threads

½ teaspoon ground cinnamon

1 teaspoon ground ginger

1 teaspoon ground turmeric

3 tablespoons olive oil

2 tablespoons minced fresh ginger

1 cup minced onion

3 pounds lamb shoulder and neck, cut into cubes (and any extra bones you can coax from the butcher)

2 tablespoons honey

1 cup pitted prunes

¼ cup slivered almonds

There was a large and thriving Jewish population in Morocco, and their cooking was quite sophisticated. A tagine, one of Morocco's finest dishes, is both a pot and the flavorful stew cooked in it. The pot is earthenware, with a conical lid that traps steam, but the dish can be made in a heavy pot with a tight-fitting lid. There are many tagines, including fish, beef, and chicken. This lamb tagine uses lamb shoulder, though Moroccan Jews might have used leg (which Ashkenazim deem unkosher).

1. Combine the saffron, cinnamon, ground ginger, and turmeric in a mortar. With a pestle, pound until the saffron is pulverized.

2. Heat the oil in a tagine or Dutch oven. Add the spice mixture and the fresh ginger. Sauté for a moment or two. Add the onion. Stir over low heat for 2 to 3 minutes; add the meat. Turn the pieces until they are coated with the spices and are lightly browned. Add 1 cup of water, bring to boiling, and lower the heat. Add any extra bones, which will give volume and flavor to the dish. Cover the pot with aluminum foil and then its cover; simmer for 40 minutes.

3. Add the honey and the prunes, replace the lid, and cook gently for another 20 to 30 minutes, until the lamb is tender and the prunes are plump.

4. Toast the almonds in a dry skillet.

5. Just before serving, remove and discard the extra bones, place the lamb on a platter, and remove as much fat as you can from the sauce. Surround the meat with prune sauce, and sprinkle with almonds.

AHEAD OF TIME NOTE:
If you make the tagine well in advance of serving, store the sauce and the meat separately in the refrigerator. The fat will harden on top of the sauce, making it easy to remove.

LAMB WITH HONEY

Before the Inquisition there were large Jewish and Moorish populations in Spain during the years of benevolent Moorish rule from the eighth to the fifteenth centuries. Both populations were forbidden pork, so they ate lamb, mutton, and some beef. It is likely that this ancient Spanish recipe was enjoyed by both the Jews and the Arabs. It's best served with rice or boiled potatoes.

3 tablespoons olive oil

2 cups chopped onion

1 cup minced green pepper

1 teaspoon paprika

4 pounds lamb stew meat (with bone)

½ cup dry red wine

Pinch of saffron threads

Salt

Freshly ground black pepper

3 tablespoons wine vinegar

2 tablespoons honey

1. Heat the oil in a large Dutch oven or other stew pot. Add the onion and green pepper. Sauté slowly for 10 minutes, until softened. Stir in the paprika.

2. Move the vegetables to the side of the pan and add the lamb; stir to brown. It won't be evenly colored, but it should lose its raw cast.

3. Add the wine, ½ cup water, saffron, salt, and pepper. Bring to simmering, cover the pot, and cook slowly for 1 to 1½ hours, until the lamb is tender.

4. Stir in the wine vinegar and honey and cook slowly for another 10 minutes.

AHEAD OF TIME NOTE:

Like most stews, this one is better the day after it's made. Reheat gently before serving.

CHOLENT

*Ye shall kindle no fire
throughout your habitations
upon the Sabbath day.*

EXODUS 35:3

THOUGH THE QUOTE THAT OPENS THIS chapter may have referred to the fire of anger or controversy, which has no place on Shabbat, it has come to be interpreted literally to mean no cooking fire may be lit (nor electric lights). The long-cooked stews were created to observe this restriction. Cholent (eastern Europe), also called schalet (western Europe); dafina, adafina, and hamin (North Africa); and hameen (India), is a universal Sabbath dish and the food most representative of the day. Heinrich Heine, the nineteenth-century German-Jewish poet, referred to schalet as "God's kosher ambrosia."

Though Jewish law prohibits work and the lighting of a fire on the Sabbath, it is nonetheless a mitzvah to have a hot meal. The restrictions on cooking derive from a phrase in the Talmud that occurs in the Friday-evening service. This ninth-century Mishnah instructs that the hot things be "hidden or covered." The Hebrew phrase was *toemnin et hahamin,* from which comes *hamin.* Raymond Sokolov, in *The Jewish-American Kitchen,* tells us that all the words for cholent throughout the Diaspora are translations from the original Hebrew-Aramaic words meaning "hidden" or "hot." In many eastern European countries, the entire village placed its cholent pots in the baker's oven, which retained enough heat to cook them over Friday night.

The recipes that follow derive from both Ashkenazic and Sephardic traditions. All are suitable for long, slow cooking in a low oven or on a *blech* or heavy flame-tamer on top of the stove. If you like, they can also be served for Friday dinner, after four to five hours of cooking.

CHOLENT

This is a typical eastern European cholent.

1. Dry the meat with a paper towel. In a heavy pot, brown the meat on all sides over high heat in the oil.

2. Add the onion and paprika. Stir for 5 minutes or so, until the onion softens.

3. Add the remaining ingredients and enough cold water to almost cover the contents. Bring to boiling, reduce the heat, and skim off the foam as it rises. Partially cover the pot and simmer very gently (over a *blech* or flame-tamer) for about 2 hours.

4. Preheat the oven to 225 to 250 degrees. Just before sundown, check to make sure the ingredients are barely covered by liquid, and put the cholent in the oven until lunch on Saturday (16 to 20 hours).

3½-pound beef chuck, in one piece

4 tablespoons vegetable oil

4 cups coarsely chopped onion

1 tablespoon paprika

1 cup red kidney beans, washed

⅓ cup barley

2 cups coarsely chopped carrot

4 garlic cloves, peeled

2 pounds potatoes, cubed

Salt

Freshly ground black pepper

SANDRA GLUCK'S "QUICK" CHOLENT

⅔ cup white or red kidney beans, picked over

⅔ cup baby lima beans, picked over

2 tablespoons vegetable oil

5 pounds well-trimmed short ribs or flanken, cut into 3-inch lengths

2 cups chopped onion

5 garlic cloves, peeled and slivered

1 cup thinly sliced carrots

1½ teaspoons sweet paprika

1 teaspoon ground ginger or 1 tablespoon grated fresh ginger

½ teaspoon sugar

¾ teaspoon dried thyme

¾ teaspoon ground cinnamon

½ teaspoon freshly ground black pepper

¼ teaspoon ground cloves

½ cup coarsely chopped pitted prunes

3 tablespoons pearl barley

1 pound all-purpose potatoes, peeled and cut into ½-inch chunks

1½ teaspoons salt

Freshly ground black pepper

3 tablespoons fine bread crumbs (optional)

Sandra Gluck is a New York chef and writer. And what a cook she is! When I told her about my book, she sent this cholent recipe. It cooks for only 2½ to 3 hours. You can, of course, cook it for the traditional 16 hours in the oven at a lower temperature. I've adapted Sandy's recipe slightly.

1. Soak the kidney beans and lima beans in a large bowl with water to cover for 8 hours or overnight.

2. When you're ready to make the cholent, heat the oil in a large Dutch oven in which all the ingredients will fit. Add as much meat as will fit comfortably in one layer and brown on all sides. Remove the meat to a platter as each batch is done. Repeat until all the meat is brown. Pour most of the fat out of the pot.

3. Preheat the oven to 350 degrees for "quick" cooking; 250 degrees for traditional slow cooking.

4. Add the onion and garlic to the pot and sauté, stirring frequently, until the onion is soft, about 10 minutes. Stir in the carrot and continue to sauté, stirring frequently, until softened, about 5 minutes more. Stir in the paprika, ginger, sugar, thyme, cinnamon, pepper, and cloves. Add the prunes, barley, drained beans, potatoes, and meat. Season with salt. Add 4 cups of water and stir.

5. Bring to boiling on top of the stove, reduce the heat so the liquid is simmering, and cover the pot. Transfer the pot to the oven and cook for 1½ to 2 hours at the higher temperature or 14 to 16 hours at the lower temperature.

6. Like cassoulet, the dish may be uncovered, sprinkled with dry bread crumbs, and baked 20 minutes longer. This will yield an appealing crust.

DAFINA (MOROCCAN CHOLENT)

Serves 8

The flavors of North Africa are very seductive in this cholent.

1. Preheat the oven to 250 degrees.

2. Cover the chickpeas with water and bring to boiling. Cover the pot, remove from heat, and set them aside while you prepare the rest of the ingredients.

3. Heat the oil in a 4-quart Dutch oven or skillet large enough to hold all the ingredients. Sauté the onion for a few minutes, until softened. Stir in the turmeric, cinnamon, ginger, saffron, and cumin. Sauté for just a minute or two. Add the remaining ingredients, including the drained chickpeas, but not the eggs, along with 6 to 7 cups of water — the ingredients should be barely covered with liquid. Bring to boiling. Gently press the eggs into the stew.

4. Cover the pan tightly, place it in the preheated oven, and bake for 12 to 16 hours.

5. When you're ready to serve, shell the eggs, slice them, and use them to garnish the dafina.

1 cup dried chickpeas

2 tablespoons olive or vegetable oil

3 cups chopped onion

1 teaspoon turmeric

½ teaspoon cinnamon

1 teaspoon grated fresh ginger

½ teaspoon saffron, crushed

1 tablespoon toasted cumin seeds, ground (see Note, page 123)

3 pounds boned lamb shoulder or beef chuck roast, brisket, or other pot roast, cut into large chunks

1 cup lentils, picked over and washed

1 cup fine egg noodles

½ cup chopped dried dates

1 tablespoon salt

Freshly ground black pepper

8 eggs

Cholent

155

MEATLESS CHOLENT

2 tablespoons vegetable oil

2 cups coarsely chopped onion

1 cup barley

1 cup split peas, picked over

2 cups coarsely chopped carrot

2 pounds all-purpose potatoes, peeled and cut into large dice

½ cup coarsely chopped parsnip

1 vegetable broth cube, diluted with 6 cups water

Salt

Freshly ground black pepper

Observant vegetarians will appreciate this dish. It's also good as an accompaniment to plain roast chicken or broiled lamb chops.

1. Heat the oil in a heavy skillet and sauté the onion until softened, about 10 minutes.

2. Add the remaining ingredients, reserving any liquid that may not fit in the pot, but do make sure the ingredients are barely covered. Bring to boiling, skim any foam that rises, partially cover the pot, and simmer very slowly on a *blech* or flame-tamer for 1½ to 2 hours.

3. Preheat the oven to 250 degrees. Just before sundown, check to see that the ingredients are barely covered with liquid. Cover the pan tightly and place it in the oven until you are ready to eat the cholent for lunch on Saturday (16 to 20 hours).

PHYLLIS GLAZER'S VEGETARIAN CHOLENT

Phyllis Glazer is an American food journalist living in Israel. This is my adaptation of her delicious cholent.

1. Wash the chickpeas and place them in a saucepan with plenty of water. Bring to a vigorous boil, cover the pot, turn off the heat, and let sit for 1 hour.

2. In a large, heavy Dutch oven with a tight-fitting lid, sauté the onion in the oil until nicely colored. Add the honey and cook until the onion is brown; be careful not to burn the onion.

3. Place the drained chickpeas, onion, lentils, barley, cumin, coriander, salt, and pepper in a mixing bowl. Line the pot in which you cooked the onion with a layer of potato slices. Add the remaining potatoes to the mixing bowl with the rest of the ingredients. Mix well and add to the pot.

4. Preheat the oven to 275 degrees.

5. Wash the eggs and pierce them, top and bottom, with a straight pin. Bury them in the ingredients in the pot. Add 4 cups water, bring to boiling, cover, and simmer for 15 minutes. Place the pot in the oven for 12 to 16 hours. Check before sundown to make sure there's enough water. Serve for Saturday lunch.

¾ cup dried chickpeas, picked over (not canned)

2 cups thickly sliced onion

2 tablespoons peanut oil

1 tablespoon honey

½ cup lentils, picked over and washed

½ cup pearl barley

2 tablespoons toasted cumin seeds, ground (see Note, page 123)

1 tablespoon ground coriander seed

2 tablespoons salt

1 tablespoon freshly ground black pepper

1 to 1½ pounds potatoes, thickly sliced (peeling is optional)

6 fresh eggs

CHOLENT GONEF

¼ cup chicken, goose, or
   duck fat (pages 36 and
   120)

 2 cups minced onion

½ cup minced celery

½ cup grated carrot

⅓ cup grated potato or
   cooked pearl barley

⅔ cup all-purpose flour
   Salt
   Freshly ground black
   pepper

¼ cup toasted bread crumbs

 1 egg, lightly beaten

The *gonef* (Yiddish for "thief") was used to "steal" the flavor from the simmering cholent and stretch the meal. It was an in-expensive "extender"; a shtetl Hamburger Helper. The gonef used some of the same ingredients as *helzel,* stuffed chicken neck, and *kishke,* stuffed derma. The derma is beef casing, the small intestine of a cow, and cleaning it is not such a pleasant task. The cheesecloth method allows the flavors of the cholent to penetrate the gonef. This is good with all the cholents in the chapter.

1. Heat the fat in a skillet. Sauté the onion until soft but not colored, about 15 minutes. Add the celery and carrot and cook for 5 minutes more. Off the heat, add the potato or barley.

2. Wash a piece of cheesecloth about 2 feet long in cold water and wring it out. Place the cheesecloth on the counter in front of you.

3. Sift the flour with the salt and pepper directly into the skil-let. Add the bread crumbs and stir to combine. Stir in the egg.

4. Scoop the gonef ingredients onto the cheesecloth, making a thin cylinder. Fold the cheesecloth loosely over the gonef, tying it in several places, like a sausage, to keep the ingredi-ents from spilling out. Place the gonef on top of cholent just before you put it in the oven. Unwrap it when you serve the cholent and spoon it into a serving bowl.

VARIATION:

For helzel, stuff the mixture into the skin of a chicken or goose, sew it up, and roast it in a 350-degree oven or poach it in chicken or meat stock. You can also poach the gonef, in cheesecloth or poultry skin, in simmering chicken soup or meat stock.

POTATOES,
NOODLES,
RICE, AND
GRAINS

───◆◆◆───

For the Lord thy God bringeth thee into a
good land . . . of wheat and barley, and vines
and fig trees and pomegranates; a land of
olive tress and honey; a land wherein thou
shalt eat bread without scarceness.

DEUTERONOMY 8:7–9

───◆◆◆───

GRAINS WERE KNOWN IN BIBLICAL
times; the potato, of course, came from the New World and sus-
tained the poor Jews of eastern Europe for much of the nineteenth century; and Jews were probably introduced to rice
during the Babylonian exile. It was most likely brought from
Asia to Persia three thousand years ago. In the eighth century
Arabs introduced rice to Spain, where it became a mainstay of
Sephardic cooking.

Recipes in this chapter are side dishes, to be served hot with
main courses. Elsewhere, there are recipes that incorporate rice
(see Poultry, page 87), lentils (see Fish, page 63), and chickpeas
(see Soups, page 43; Fish; and Meat, page 121), as an integral part
of a dish or as a salad (see Salads, page 213).

MASHED POTATOES

Serves 6

These dairy-free potatoes are simple and delicious. No one will miss the butter and milk. They're best made just before serving.

1. Peel and cube the potatoes. Boil them with the onion and garlic for 15 to 20 minutes.

2. Drain the vegetables. Put them through a potato ricer or food mill directly into the serving bowl. Season with salt and pepper and stir in the olive oil. Sprinkle with parsley and serve.

3 pounds potatoes, all-purpose, russet, or new

2 cups chopped onion

6 to 8 garlic cloves, peeled
Salt
Freshly ground black pepper

4 tablespoons olive oil

4 tablespoons minced parsley

Potatoes, Noodles, Rice, and Grains

161

Makes about 40 3- to 4-inch pancakes; serves 8 to 10

POTATO LATKES

6 large Idaho potatoes,
9 to 10 ounces each

3 medium onions

4 eggs, lightly beaten

¼ to ½ cup flour

2 tablespoons salt

Freshly ground black
pepper

Peanut oil for frying

Latkes are particularly special on Hanukkah, which in some years spans two Fridays. The oil in which the latkes fry commemorates the oil that lit the Temple after its recapture by Judas Maccabaeus in 165. B.C.E.

Latkes are a commitment. You can't expect them to be crisp and delicious if you make them far in advance, so you must stand and fry while others enjoy the meal. The cook's reward is latkes right out of the pan.

1. Peel the potatoes and onions. Chop them in pieces small enough to fit through the feed tube of a food processor, if you are using one. Grate them with the small-hole grater attachment; alternatively, you can pulse them with the steel blade. But be careful not to overprocess or you'll get a gluey mess. If you're grating the potatoes and onions by hand, leave them whole and grate them on the largest holes of a box grater. Transfer the grated potatoes and onions to a sieve set over a large bowl. Press down with a wooden spoon to release the liquid into the bowl. With your hands, squeeze the remaining moisture out of the potatoes and spread them out on paper towels.

2. Put the potatoes and onions in another large bowl. Pour off any liquid given off by the draining potatoes, reserving the heavy starch that remains in the bottom of the draining bowl. Transfer the starch to the potatoes and onions.

3. Add the eggs to the potatoes and onions, along with ¼ cup of flour and the salt and pepper. Mix completely with your scrupulously clean hands or a wooden spoon.

4. Heat ¼ inch of oil in a large heavy frying pan. When it's almost smoking, add the batter by tablespoonsful, pressing down to flatten them. I like small, flat, crisp latkes, but others prefer larger, thicker ones. Adjust the quantity of batter to your taste, pressing down or not. Don't crowd the pan. As each batch is done, transfer it to a paper towel–lined platter and serve. If you must, you can keep them warm for 30 minutes or so in a 200-degree oven without doing too much damage.

AHEAD OF TIME NOTE:

You can make the batter an hour or two in advance of frying. Sprinkle the top with flour to keep the batter from turning altogether brown.

ROASTED POTATO "FRIES"

2 pounds new white or red potatoes

4 tablespoons olive oil

1 garlic clove, peeled and sliced

1 tablespoon rosemary

Salt

Freshly ground black pepper

These simple potatoes are crispy on the outside and soft within. Delicious!

1. Preheat the oven to 400 degrees.

2. Cover the potatoes with salted water and boil until barely tender, about 10 minutes.

3. Drain the potatoes and cut them into 2-inch cubes, more or less. (Peeling is optional.) Pat dry.

4. Heat the oil in a cast-iron skillet or other heavy pan that can go into the oven. Add the garlic and rosemary and stir for a moment.

5. Add the potatoes, season with salt and pepper, and toss to combine. Roast in the oven for 45 to 60 minutes, stirring from time to time. The potatoes will be crisp and brown.

AHEAD OF TIME NOTE:

The potatoes can be parboiled and cubed in advance. You can set them aside at room temperature for a few hours or overnight in the refrigerator before continuing.

SABBATH SAFFRON RICE

Edda Servi Machlin, in her excellent book *The Classic Cuisine of the Italian Jews,* describes this *risi gialli,* yellow rice, as the "Jewish dish par excellence." Saffron, she states, is thought to have been brought to Ferrara from Asia Minor by the Jews for this Sabbath rice.

1. Mrs. Machlin flavors her oil before using it in this splendid dish. Heat the olive oil with the garlic, rosemary, salt, and pepper. Cook over medium heat until the garlic is colored, about 15 minutes. Add a few drops of water; remove from the heat and let cool. Strain the oil and discard the contents of the strainer.

2. Place the rice in a heavy saucepan with 6 tablespoons of the flavored oil (save any remaining oil for other cooking). Cook, stirring, for about 3 minutes. Add 1 cup of the hot broth and cook, covered, over medium heat, for 5 minutes, or until most of the liquid is absorbed by the rice. Add a second cup of broth and continue to cook, covered, until the rice is again almost dry. Add the saffron to the third cup of liquid; add to the rice and cook for a final 5 to 8 minutes. You may need up to 1 additional cup liquid if the rice isn't fully cooked. Add salt and pepper and mix. Spread on a flat dish to cool. Serve warm or at room temperature.

½ cup olive oil

1 large garlic clove, peeled

Small branch fresh rosemary or 1 teaspoon dried

2 teaspoons salt

¼ teaspoon freshly ground black pepper

1½ cups long-grain uncooked white rice

3 to 4 cups hot chicken stock

⅛ teaspoon crushed saffron

Potatoes, Noodles, Rice, and Grains

165

RICE AND ORZO

2 tablespoons vegetable oil

¼ cup orzo

1 cup uncooked white rice

1 teaspoon salt

Freshly ground black pepper

Rae Dayan is a renowned Syrian-Jewish home cook in Brooklyn. This delicious recipe, wonderful with roasts and chicken, is adapted from her cookbook *For the Love of Cooking,* published in a ring binder, distributed by the Sephardic Community Center in Brooklyn.

Heat the oil in a heavy skillet. Sauté the orzo until lightly colored — this makes the finished dish look like it's filled with almonds and creates a nice contrast to the rice. Stir in the rice and sauté for a moment. Add 2 cups of water and bring to boiling. Add the salt, stir, cover, and simmer for 20 minutes. Fluff the rice and orzo with a fork, grind some pepper over it, and serve.

AHEAD OF TIME NOTE:

If the rice must wait, turn off the heat, cover it with a terry cloth dish towel, and replace the cover. The rice will stay warm for at least 30 minutes.

RICE AND
CHICKPEAS

Here's another Syrian-Jewish dish. It's good with stews and lamb shanks and roast chicken.

Heat the oil in a large saucepan and sauté the garlic and onion until the onion softens. Add the rice, stirring to combine with the onion, garlic, and oil. Pour in the boiling water, stir, and add the chickpeas and salt. Stir again. Cover and simmer for 30 minutes. Fluff with a fork and serve.

AHEAD OF TIME NOTE:

You can make this an hour or so in advance. Cover the saucepan with a kitchen towel, replace the cover, and keep on a flame-tamer over very low heat.

- 2 tablespoons olive or vegetable oil
- 2 tablespoons minced garlic
- 2 cups chopped onion
- 1 cup uncooked white rice
- 2 cups boiling water
- 1 15-ounce can chickpeas, drained and rinsed
- 2 teaspoons salt

Potatoes, Noodles, Rice, and Grains

KASHA

1 egg

1 cup whole-grain kasha
(see Note)

Salt

2 cups chicken stock or
water

2 tablespoons shmaltz
(page 36), butter, or
margarine

Kasha is the Russian word for cereal, but this classic eastern European dish is the milled form of grain buckwheat. Because it grows in areas generally too cold for wheat, it was a staple of Russians and Poles, Jews and non-Jews alike.

1. Beat the egg just to combine the white and yolk. Stir in the kasha and a good pinch of salt.

2. Heat a heavy skillet, preferably cast iron, though enameled cast iron will do. Toast the groats over medium heat until the grains start to separate and give off a nutty smell. Stir frequently, scraping the bottom of the pan. Toast until the kasha kernels are separate, but don't burn them.

3. Heat the stock or water in a saucepan with a cover. When it boils, slowly stir in the groats. Add the fat. Cover the pan tightly and cook over the lowest possible heat for 15 to 20 minutes, until the liquid is absorbed. The kasha can be cooked for the same amount of time in a preheated 350-degree oven.

4. Fluff the kasha with a fork and serve. If you want the kasha to wait, cover the pan with a folded dish towel and keep it warm in a 250-degree oven. The kasha will improve.

NOTE:

Use only whole buckwheat groats, not medium or fine, which will yield a gruel-like porridge.

VARIATION:

Hot kasha makes a fine light lunch if you add sautéed mushrooms. If the meal is a dairy one, add sour cream for a real treat.

KASHA VARNISHKES

Varnishkes means "boil" in Russian, and that's what you do to the noodles that create this classic dish.

1. Cook the onion slowly in the fat for 15 to 20 minutes, until soft but not colored.

2. Cook the noodles in a large quantity of boiling water for 10 minutes. Drain.

3. Combine the noodles, onion, and kasha in a large bowl and serve.

AHEAD OF TIME NOTE:

If a wait is required, put the kasha varnishkes in a pan, cover with a dish towel, and keep warm over a flame-tamer for up to 1 hour. If a longer wait is needed, put the kasha varnishkes in a greased ovenproof dish and reheat it in a 325-degree oven for 20 to 25 minutes.

1 cup chopped onion

1 tablespoon shmaltz (page 36), butter, or margarine

1 cup (2 ounces) bow tie–shaped egg noodles

2 cups hot Kasha (made from 1 cup raw, see recipe opposite)

FARFEL

2 cups minced onion

2 tablespoons vegetable oil

½ pound mushrooms, wiped and chopped (3 to 3½ cups)

2 cups farfel (egg barley)

2 cups chicken soup or water

Salt

Freshly ground black pepper

Farfel is an Ashkenazic egg noodle known as egg barley, probably because of its shape. In eastern Europe it was made with scraps of Friday's challah. The dough was torn or chopped into very small pieces and rolled between the fingers or grated on a rough grater, which created irregular crumbs. It makes a delicious side dish. It could be tricky trying to buy farfel in your supermarket: Mother's makes something called "barley shape" enriched egg noodle product; Goodman's markets their product as "egg flakes" enriched egg noodle product. The Goodman's is in the shape of little squares, but it's fine for these recipes.

FARFEL AND MUSHROOMS

1. Preheat the oven to 325 degrees.

2. In a large skillet, sauté the onion in the oil, stirring until the onion is soft and just taking on color, about 15 minutes.

3. Add the mushrooms and continue sautéing until the mushrooms give up their liquid. Stir in the farfel, chicken soup or water, salt, and pepper. Bring to simmering.

4. Transfer the mixture to a 6-cup shallow baking pan. Bake in the oven for 30 to 40 minutes, until the liquid is absorbed and the farfel is soft and done. Remove the farfel from the oven and serve.

AHEAD OF TIME NOTE:
The farfel can be made ahead and reheated in a 300-degree oven for about 20 minutes; add more liquid if it seems dry.

SIMPLE FARFEL

The toasted farfel, onions, and shmaltz make this dish far from simple in taste.

1. Preheat the oven to 350 degrees. Bring a large quantity of salted water to boiling.

2. Spread the farfel on a baking sheet or in a shallow skillet and place it in the oven for 15 to 20 minutes, stirring from time to time to ensure even browning.

3. Transfer the toasted farfel to the boiling water and cook for 10 minutes; drain.

4. Sauté the onion in the shmaltz or oil until soft but barely colored. Add the farfel, salt, and pepper; stir, heat, and serve.

Serves 6

2 cups farfel (egg barley)

2 cups chopped onion

3 tablespoons shmaltz (page 36) or vegetable oil

Salt

Freshly ground black pepper

MUSHROOM-BARLEY PILAF

- 4 tablespoons olive oil or butter
- 8 to 10 scallions, minced, including 2 inches of greens
- ½ pound mushrooms, cleaned and chopped (3 to 3½ cups)
- 1 cup pearl barley, rinsed
- 3 cups vegetable broth or water, boiling (see Note)
  Freshly ground black pepper
  Salt
- ½ cup chopped parsley

Mushroom-Barley Soup (page 59) is a staple of eastern European–inspired Jewish cooking. This casserole makes an excellent vegetarian entrée. It's also good as a side dish with fish or chicken.

1. Preheat the oven to 350 degrees.

2. Heat the oil or butter in a saucepan and add the scallions, mushrooms, and barley. Cook for 5 to 8 minutes, until the mushrooms give up their liquid.

3. Add the boiling broth, pepper, and salt. Transfer the mixture to a shallow 2-quart casserole dish. Bake for 45 to 50 minutes, until the liquid is absorbed. Stir before serving, sprinkled with parsley.

NOTE:

I dilute a vegetable broth cube in 3 cups of hot water. Do this in a measuring cup and mash the cube against the sides with a wooden spoon. You can combine the hot, rather than boiling, broth with the barley.

MAMALIGA

Mamaliga is Romanian polenta, the lovely Italian cornmeal mush. Moldavians claim theirs is better than the Italians' because it's made from local stone-ground orange cornmeal. The Italians are probably unaware that they have any competition for their justifiably famous comfort food. Here in America we also have excellent stone-ground cornmeal — look for it when you make this dish. Don't use "instant," because the results will be less satisfactory.

This is a wonderful accompaniment to such hearty dishes as Winter Beef Stew (page 128) and Braised Short Ribs (page 126).

4 to 5 cups boiling water
1 teaspoon salt
1 cup cornmeal
4 tablespoons butter or olive oil

1. In a large heavy pot, combine 3 cups of the boiling water and the salt. Slowly stir in the cornmeal. Over low heat, keep stirring the mamaliga until it's a thick porridge and no longer grainy; this will take up to 30 minutes, depending on the type and age of the cornmeal. Add more simmering water as necessary.

2. Stir in the butter or oil. Pour the mamaliga into a bowl and serve it immediately, or pour it onto a large platter, cool, cut it into strips, and grill or fry it.

AHEAD OF TIME NOTE:

You can make the mamaliga up to 45 minutes before serving. Keep it warm in a double boiler over simmering water.

KUGELS

Even if the kugel doesn't quite work out,
you still have the noodles.

SHOLOM ALEICHEM

A KUGEL IS A PUDDING, SWEET OR SAVORY. The word *kugel* in German means "globe" or "ball." Perhaps the pudding is the Yiddish abbreviation of kugelhof, popular yeast breads found in southwest Germany, Alsace, and Austria. Possibly it was the round form of these yeast breads, studded with raisins, that evolved into the Jewish pudding. Kugels are a constant feature for Shabbat and holidays.

Lokshen, or noodle, kugels are classics, a standard of Ashkenazic cooking. They combine noodles, fat, eggs, and seasoning. Those suitable for dairy meals often include cheese and butter. In Lithuania and other eastern European countries, after separating the challah, women would remove another piece of the egg dough and roll it into noodles. Some were used in the Friday-night soup, some were used to make a kugel for Saturday lunch, some were dried and used during the week.

Potatoes were a staple of eastern European Jews in the nineteenth century. Cheap and easily obtainable, potatoes mature in two or three months instead of the six to ten months required to ripen grain. Only the Irish were as dependent on potatoes. Poor eastern European Jews ate potatoes sometimes twice a day and developed a rich potato repertoire, including kugels.

DAIRY LOKSHEN KUGEL/1

We always had a version of this kugel as part of our Yom Kippur break fast. But it's too good for just a once-a-year outing. It's a fine Shabbat dish to accompany fish or a vegetarian meal.

1. Preheat the oven to 350 degrees. With a little of the melted butter, brush a shallow 3-quart ovenproof dish.

2. Bring a large quantity of water to boiling. Add salt and the noodles. Cook for about 10 minutes, until the noodles are tender. Drain.

3. In a large bowl, combine the cottage cheese, sour cream, eggs, sugar, currants or raisins, and apple. Mix well. Add the noodles and mix again. Turn the mixture into the prepared dish.

4. Combine the bread crumbs with all but 1 tablespoon of the remaining butter, the cinnamon, and the brown sugar. Spread this over the pudding and drizzle the top with the remaining butter. Bake the kugel for 45 minutes to an hour, until the top is brown and the kugel bubbling.

NOTE:
Some people top the kugel with crushed cornflakes.

6 tablespoons butter, melted

Salt

1 pound broad egg noodles

2 cups cottage cheese

2 cups sour cream

4 eggs, lightly beaten

½ cup sugar

½ cup currants or raisins

1 cup peeled and minced Granny Smith apple

1 cup plain white bread crumbs (see Note)

1 teaspoon ground cinnamon

1 teaspoon brown sugar

Kugels

DAIRY LOKSHEN KUGEL/2

8 tablespoons (1 stick) butter, melted

Salt

½ pound thin egg noodles

3 eggs

3½ ounces cream cheese

½ cup sugar

1 teaspoon vanilla extract

Salt

¾ cup sour cream

½ cup milk

1 teaspoon ground cinnamon

Grated peel and juice from 1 lemon

Here's another good kugel for no-meat meals.

1. Preheat the oven to 350 degrees. Brush a 2-quart ovenproof dish with a little of the melted butter.

2. Bring a large quantity of water to boiling. Add 1 tablespoon salt and the noodles. Cook the noodles for 3 to 4 minutes, until tender. Drain.

3. In a large bowl, beat the eggs. Add the remaining ingredients, combining them well. Finally, add the cooked noodles and mix well. Turn the mixture into the prepared pan and bake it for 35 to 45 minutes, until the top is lightly brown and the kugel is firm.

JERUSALEM KUGEL

Dahlia Carmel, the indispensable friend to all cookbook writers and herself a major cookbook collector, told me about Jerusalem kugel when I mentioned I was writing this book. Several recipes arrived in the mail, and here's my version. Dahlia says, "Don't forget to eat it with pickles."

½ cup vegetable oil

½ cup sugar

Salt

12 ounces fine egg noodles

4 eggs, lightly beaten

2 teaspoons freshly ground black pepper

1. Preheat the oven to 350 degrees. Bring a large quantity of water to boiling.

2. Heat the vegetable oil in a saucepan. Add the sugar and, stirring constantly for 10 minutes over low heat, let it brown. The mixture will not amalgamate, but the sugar should dissolve.

3. Salt the water and add the noodles. They should cook in 3 to 5 minutes. Drain.

4. Taking care, for the sugar will spatter, add the noodles to the sugar. Add the eggs and the pepper. Mix well. Taste for seasoning. The kugel should be peppery and well salted. Transfer the kugel to a 6-cup soufflé tin or other ovenproof dish of the same capacity. A wide shallow dish will give you crunchy noodles and a dry interior texture; a soufflé dish will yield a crunchy top and a moist interior.

5. Place the kugel in the oven for 2 hours. Check from time to time to make sure the kugel browns but doesn't burn. Cover it with parchment or aluminum foil if it starts to burn.

6. After 2 hours, remove the kugel from the oven. Run a spatula around the sides of the baking dish and unmold the kugel by turning it upside down on a plate. You may have to tap the bottom of the pan, but it should come out. If it doesn't, serve it from the pan.

LOKSHEN KUGEL
(MEAT)

⅓ cup shmaltz (page 36) or goose fat (page 120), melted

2 cups minced onion

Salt

½ pound medium egg noodles

3 eggs

Gribenes (optional) (page 36)

Freshly ground black pepper

This is a traditional nondairy kugel. Though the eggs, gribenes, and shmaltz may seem excessive, the kugel is shared by eight people, so it's not all that much per person.

1. Preheat the oven to 375 degrees. Brush a shallow 2-quart ovenproof dish with 1 tablespoon of the shmaltz or goose fat.

2. Cook the onion slowly in the remaining shmaltz until soft, about 15 minutes.

3. While the onion cooks, bring a large quantity of water to boiling. Add salt and the noodles. Boil for 7 to 10 minutes, until the noodles are tender.

4. Beat the eggs just to combine in a large mixing bowl. Add the noodles and the onion, along with the fat in which they cooked, and the gribenes, salt, and pepper; mix well. Turn the mixture into the prepared pan and bake for 30 to 40 minutes, until the kugel is lightly brown.

POTATO, TURNIP, AND BROCCOLI KUGEL

This kugel was an experiment because I had potatoes, a few turnips, and broccoli that were not getting any younger. It's very good with olive oil or shmaltz, but the goose fat makes it really special.

1. Cover the potatoes and turnips with cold water, bring to boiling, and cook for 20 to 40 minutes, until the vegetables are completely tender. Drain. When cool enough to handle, peel the potatoes and mash them with the turnip in a bowl with a potato masher; alternatively, put them through a food mill. A food processor will turn them gluey.

2. Preheat the oven to 350 degrees.

3. Peel the broccoli stems and slice them thickly; trim the florets and cut them into small pieces. Put the broccoli into a large quantity of salted boiling water and cook for about 5 to 6 minutes — it should be crisp-tender.

4. Heat 3 tablespoons of the fat or oil in a skillet; sauté the onion for 15 to 20 minutes, until completely soft and turning brown.

5. Combine the potatoes, turnips, and onion. Add salt, pepper, and the egg; mix well. Add the broccoli and mix again.

6. Turn the mixture into a 6-cup ovenproof dish, dot the top with the remaining fat or oil. Cook the kugel in the preheated oven for 45 minutes, until it is firm and golden.

AHEAD OF TIME NOTE:

This kugel can be prepared, through step 5, hours in advance; once baked it should be served immediately.

2 pounds potatoes, quartered

½ pound turnips (2 small), peeled and quartered

1½ pounds broccoli (about 3 large stalks)

5 tablespoons rendered goose fat (page 120), shmaltz (page 36), or olive oil

2 cups chopped onion

Salt

Freshly ground black pepper

1 egg, lightly beaten

Serves 8 to 10

POTATO AND
PARSNIP KUGEL

3 pounds potatoes

1 to 1½ pounds parsnips

6 tablespoons shmaltz
(page 36), duck or goose
fat (page 120), olive oil,
or vegetable oil

4 cups coarsely chopped
onion

3 eggs, lightly beaten

Nutmeg

Salt

Freshly ground black
pepper

1 tablespoon bread crumbs
or matzo meal

Parsnips have a lovely sweet taste but not much romance. They're delicious roasted, and wonderful in this kugel with potatoes.

1. Quarter the potatoes and the parsnips. Boil them in water to cover for 15 to 20 minutes, until both are tender. Drain.

2. Heat 3 tablespoons of the shmaltz, fat, or oil in a skillet. Sauté the onion slowly for 15 to 20 minutes, until very soft and only lightly colored.

3. Preheat the oven to 400 degrees. Grease a 2-quart shallow casserole or gratin dish with 1 tablespoon of the remaining shmaltz or oil.

4. Peel and chop the potatoes. Put them through a food mill fitted with the coarse blade, along with the parsnips and onion. Don't use a food processor, which will create a glue-like mass.

5. Stir in the eggs and a few gratings of nutmeg. Taste, and add as much salt and pepper as you think it needs. If you don't want to taste raw eggs, taste the kugel before you add them.

6. Turn the mixture into the prepared dish and sprinkle with the bread crumbs or matzo meal; drizzle the last 2 tablespoons of shmaltz or oil over the kugel. Bake in the preheated oven for 40 to 50 minutes, until the top is golden.

AHEAD OF TIME NOTE:
You can prepare the dish in advance up to sprinkling it with the bread crumbs and the final drizzle of shmaltz, fat, or oil. The kugel is best served hot from the oven, so try not to reheat it.

VARIATION:
Substitute celery root for the parsnip — the result is a piquant and flavorful kugel.

SALT AND PEPPER NOODLE KUGEL

This is a very simple kugel; easy to make, satisfying to eat.

1. Bring 6 to 8 quarts of water to boiling. Preheat the oven to 375 degrees.

2. Salt the water and cook the noodles for 3 to 4 minutes, until soft. Drain.

3. Combine the drained noodles with the oil, salt, and pepper. Place the mixture in a 1-quart shallow gratin dish or casserole and cook in the preheated oven for 30 to 40 minutes, until a nice crust develops on the surface.

12 ounces thin egg noodles

4 tablespoons corn oil

1 tablespoon salt

½ tablespoon freshly ground black pepper

AHEAD OF TIME NOTE:

You can boil the noodles in advance. Be sure to mix them with 1 of the tablespoons of oil to prevent clumping. You can assemble the entire kugel a few hours in advance, but don't refrigerate it.

VEGETABLES

*And you shall eat
the herb of the field.*

GENESIS 3:18

THE BIBLE MENTIONS SCORES OF PLANTS, and the Talmud many more. The Mediterranean Jews were blessed with a mild climate, and they learned from Muslims in Turkey, Spain, and other parts of the medieval Muslim world about irrigation. This heritage is reflected in the enormous and varied repertoire of Sephardic vegetable dishes.

Ashkenazim, in the bleak, cold, inhospitable agricultural regions of eastern Europe, made do with cabbage, beets, carrots, parsnips, turnips, onions, and garlic.

The recipes in this chapter reflect the vast array of vegetables we have available in this country. Some are a Sephardic legacy, others Ashkenazic; some aren't specifically Jewish, just good accompaniments to the recipes throughout the book.

SAUTÉED SPINACH WITH CURRANTS AND PINE NUTS

Sephardic in inspiration, this dish is good with roast chicken and fish and even as a first course.

1. Wash and stem the spinach. You needn't dry it, but drain it well.

2. Toast the pine nuts in a cast-iron skillet. Watch carefully — they go quickly from pale to burned.

3. Heat the oil in a large skillet. Sauté the garlic for 2 to 3 minutes. Stir in the currants and then the spinach. Cover the skillet and cook for 5 minutes, until the spinach is wilted. Season with salt and pepper; toss in the pine nuts and serve.

2 pounds spinach

3 tablespoons pine nuts

2 tablespoons olive oil

1 tablespoon minced garlic

3 tablespoons currants

Salt

Freshly ground black pepper

BEET PUREE

1½ to 2 pounds beets

10 to 14 whole, unpeeled garlic cloves

3 tablespoons olive oil

2 tablespoons wine vinegar

1 tablespoon sugar

Salt

Freshly ground black pepper

I love beets: their color and their taste are enormously appealing. Here's a beautiful puree that's easy to prepare and really dramatic on the plate.

1. Roast the beets according to the directions on page 127. Wrap the garlic cloves in aluminum foil and roast them along with the beets. Cool the beets to room temperature. Peel and quarter them.

2. Put the cooked beets in a food processor. Squeeze the garlic cloves out of their skins into the processor. Add the olive oil and puree. Add the wine vinegar, sugar, salt, and pepper. Taste for seasoning.

3. Reheat the beets gently in a saucepan and serve.

AHEAD OF TIME NOTE:

You can make the puree a day in advance of serving, through step 2. Cool, cover, and refrigerate. Reheat over low heat to serve.

BRAISED LEEKS AND POTATOES

The ancient Hebrews learned about leeks from the ancient Egyptians, and it was one of the foods they yearned for during their wanderings in the wilderness (Numbers 11:5); their significance, therefore, is particularly strong at Passover. The Romans brought leeks to Britain for medicinal purposes, and there they have thrived in many recipes and as a Welsh symbol. In central and eastern Europe, leeks were called "Jewish" plants because they were used so frequently in Jewish cooking. *Prassa,* braised leeks, is a common Sephardic dish. Bert Greene, the late food writer — generous and much respected — found his recipe for *prassa* in *The Sephardic Cooks,* a book published by the Sisterhood of Congregation Or VeShalom in Atlanta, Georgia; it appears in *Greene on Greens.* Some recipes include tomatoes, some don't—this does; some include potatoes, some don't — this does. Serve as a vegetable side dish or as part of a vegetarian meal.

6 to 8 leeks

1 cup chopped onion

2 tablespoons olive oil

2 tomatoes, fresh or canned, seeded and chopped (about ½ cup)

1 teaspoon sugar

Salt

Freshly ground black pepper

1 medium potato, peeled and cubed

¼ cup chopped parsley

1. Carefully clean the leeks and cut them into 1-inch pieces, including some tender green tops.

2. Stew the leeks with the onion in the olive oil for 15 to 20 minutes, until they soften. Add the tomatoes, sugar, salt, pepper, and ½ cup water. Simmer, covered, for 15 minutes.

3. Add the potato, re-cover the pot, and cook about 20 minutes more. Sprinkle with parsley and serve.

AHEAD OF TIME NOTE:

The dish can be made in advance and reheated. If you can avoid refrigerating it, the dish will be better.

BROCCOLI PUREE

2 pounds broccoli

1 tablespoon minced garlic

2 tablespoons olive oil

Salt

Freshly ground black pepper

This is a delicious accompaniment to roast or broiled meats. It is also delicious spooned over baked potato, polenta, or rice, or as a bed on which to cook eggs. I am indebted to Viana La Place's book *Verdura* for the inspiration for this recipe.

1. Pare the broccoli stalks, shaving off the dark skin, and dice. Trim the florets; cut off any yellow or discolored parts.

2. Cover the broccoli with cold salted water and bring to boiling. Simmer for 20 minutes. Remove the broccoli, reserving the water in which it boiled.

3. On a cutting board, chop the broccoli.

4. In a skillet, slowly sauté the garlic in the oil for a few minutes; don't let it brown. Add the broccoli and a cup of the reserved cooking water. With the back of a wooden spoon, mash the broccoli from time to time. Cook for about 15 minutes, until the broccoli is a somewhat coarse puree and utterly tender. Add salt and pepper before serving.

AHEAD OF TIME NOTE:
The broccoli can be made in advance and reheated.

CARROT PUDDING

Because of their color, carrots symbolize prosperity. A carrot pudding or kugel is frequently served on Rosh Hashanah and other festive occasions. Jean Stillman, sister of my good friend Marshall Goldberg, gave me a version of this recipe for an earlier book. Here it is again, slightly altered.

1½ pounds carrots
1 tablespoon vegetable oil
4 eggs, separated
5 tablespoons brown sugar
5 tablespoons ground blanched almonds
½ cup flour
1 teaspoon salt
2 teaspoons grated lemon peel
2 tablespoons lemon juice
2 tablespoons granulated sugar

1. Scrape the carrots and cut them into thin rounds; you should have about 4 cups.

2. Cook the carrots in a large amount of boiling water until they are tender, about 15 minutes. Drain them and puree in a food processor.

3. Preheat the oven to 350 degrees. Oil a 6-cup ring mold.

4. Beat the egg yolks with the brown sugar until thick. Stir in the carrots, almonds, flour, salt, lemon peel, and lemon juice. Mix well.

5. Beat the egg whites with a pinch of salt until soft peaks form. Add the granulated sugar and beat until stiff and shiny. Fold the egg whites into the carrot mixture. Turn the pudding into the prepared ring mold, tap it lightly on the counter, and bake it for 30 to 40 minutes, until firm and lightly colored and the top is slightly cracked. Invert the ring onto a serving dish; unmold the pudding and serve it hot.

AHEAD OF TIME NOTE:
You can make the dish through step 4 several hours in advance.

CARROTS WITH GINGER AND CUMIN

1½ pounds carrots, scraped and cut into 1-inch chunks

1 tablespoon vegetable oil

4 to 6 garlic cloves, minced

2 tablespoons minced fresh ginger

1 tablespoon toasted cumin seeds, ground (see Note, page 123)

1 tablespoon freshly squeezed lemon juice

I make this dish all the time — it's utterly delicious and perks up the meal and the diners, particularly in winter.

1. Boil the carrots in salted water for about 10 minutes, until they are soft but not mushy. Timing will depend on the thickness of the carrots.

2. Heat the oil in a small sauté pan. Sauté the garlic and ginger for about 5 minutes. Add the cumin and sauté for another minute.

3. Put the carrots and the contents of the sauté pan into a food processor. Add the lemon juice and puree. Scrape down the sides of the container so the mixture is smooth. Reheat gently and serve.

AHEAD OF TIME NOTE:

This dish can easily be made in advance. It keeps in the refrigerator and reheats successfully.

CAULIFLOWER PIE

I was introduced to this recipe in Edda Servi Machlin's wonderful book *The Classic Cuisine of the Italian Jews*. The most time-consuming part of the recipe, trimming and parboiling the cauliflower, can be done well in advance of final cooking.

1. Bring a large pot of salted water to boiling.

2. Cut out the core of the cauliflower and separate the florets. Trim close to the florets and discard the stems. Add the florets to boiling water. Simmer until the cauliflower is very tender, 15 to 20 minutes. Drain in a colander and mash with a fork.

3. Heat 4 tablespoons of the olive oil in a skillet. Add the garlic and sauté slowly for 2 to 3 minutes; don't let the garlic color. Add the cauliflower, season with salt and pepper, and stir constantly over high heat until the moisture has evaporated.

4. Let the cauliflower cool for at least 15 minutes.

5. Preheat the oven to 450 degrees; oil a shallow 6-cup ovenproof pan.

6. Add the eggs and flour to the cauliflower and mix.

7. Sprinkle the prepared pan with ¼ cup of the bread crumbs. Add the cauliflower mixture and smooth it with a spatula. Top the cauliflower with the remaining bread crumbs and splash on the remaining olive oil. Bake for 30 minutes, until the top is brown and crisp. Serve immediately.

AHEAD OF TIME NOTE:

You can stop after step 3 or you can stop after assembling the pie but before baking it. Don't add the olive oil until just before baking.

1 large cauliflower, about 3 pounds

6 tablespoons olive oil

4 tablespoons minced garlic

Salt

Freshly ground black pepper

2 eggs, lightly beaten

2 tablespoons all-purpose flour

1 cup coarse bread crumbs

WHOLE CAULIFLOWER WITH PINE NUTS, CAPERS, AND VINEGAR

1 whole cauliflower, about 3 pounds

3 tablespoons pine nuts

3 tablespoons olive oil

4 garlic cloves, minced

2 tablespoons capers, rinsed and chopped

3 tablespoons wine vinegar

4 tablespoons minced parsley

This tasty dish is good with Roast Chicken (page 89), Lamb Shanks (page 145), Roast Goose (page 119), and as part of a vegetarian meal.

1. Trim the cauliflower leaves, leaving a few close to the head (for presentation). Pare the base and shave any discolored portions of the florets. Steam the whole head in a covered saucepan for 20 to 30 minutes, until tender but not mushy.

2. While the cauliflower steams, make the sauce. In a small dry skillet, toast the pine nuts. Watch them carefully, as they burn quickly. When lightly browned, remove them to a dish.

3. Heat the olive oil in the same skillet. Add the garlic and sauté for 2 to 3 minutes. Add the capers and wine vinegar. Keep the mixture warm over very low heat until the cauliflower is ready.

4. Place the tender cauliflower on a platter and pour the sauce over it. Sprinkle with toasted pine nuts and parsley. Cut into serving portions at the table.

FENNEL PUREE

This dish is simplicity itself: just salt, pepper, and fennel. It's delicious with fish or chicken or an omelet.

4 1-pound fennel bulbs
Salt
Freshly ground black pepper

1. Remove the fennel stalks close to the bulbs. Reserve a few sprigs of feathery leaves for garnishing. The stalks can be used to flavor vegetable stocks; they can also be made into a lattice-like rack for roasting fish.

2. Rinse the bulbs and peel the fibers off the outer layers with a knife. Cut the bulbs into ¼-inch-thick slices. Cover them with salted cold water, bring to boiling, and simmer for 10 to 15 minutes, under tender.

3. Drain and puree the fennel in a food processor. Drain again. Reheat the puree in a saucepan, season with salt and pepper, and serve, garnished with the reserved fronds.

AHEAD OF TIME NOTE:

The puree reheats very well. It can be made a day or two in advance and stored in the refrigerator.

GARLIC GREEN BEANS

2 pounds green beans

Salt

4 tablespoons olive oil

3 tablespoons minced garlic

Freshly ground black pepper

1 cup bread crumbs

I learned this recipe in Julia Child's 1975 book, *The Way to Cook.* Mrs. Child writes that the idea was "suggested" to her by Jacques Médecin's book *La Cuisine du Comté de Nice* (published in English as *Cuisine Niçoise*). "Suggested," she says, because she changed it around some. I changed it only a little.

1. Bring a large quantity of water to boiling.

2. Snap off the ends of the beans and cut them in half or into 1-inch lengths if they are very long.

3. Add the beans to the boiling water, sprinkle with salt (this helps set the green color), and cook for 4 to 5 minutes, until the beans are just tender. Drain; put the beans back in the pot and, shaking the pan over medium heat, dry them. Spread them on paper towels.

4. Heat the oil in a skillet and add the garlic and sauté for just a minute or two. Add the beans and toss with the oil and garlic. Cover the pan and cook over low heat for 2 to 3 minutes. Uncover, raise the heat, and stir in salt, pepper, and the bread crumbs, tossing and stirring until the crumbs turn golden and crisp, about 8 to 10 minutes. You may need to add more oil. Serve hot.

AHEAD OF TIME NOTE:

You can make the recipe through step 3 several hours in advance of serving. The beans are best served when just cooked, though they can be reheated.

GLAZED CARROTS AND PARSLEY ROOTS

1 pound carrots

1 pound parsley roots

4 tablespoons butter or olive oil

1 tablespoon sugar

Salt

Freshly ground black pepper

4 tablespoons minced parsley

This dish, delicious with fish, is inspired by the French folly Carrottes Vichy. Vichy is a spa in eastern France whose mineral water is said to have many healthful properties. You can use Vichy water for this recipe, but tap water is fine, too.

The parsley root gives a nice boost to the carrots. Parsley root that's eaten as a vegetable is especially cultivated for its root. The leaves, though abundant, are not as flavorful as the cultivated herb, whose root is small and not so good to eat.

1. Peel the carrots; quarter them lengthwise and cut into pieces 2 inches long. Do the same with the parsley roots. The thick end of the parsley roots may need to be cut in half again. Remove any woody interiors and trim the pieces so they are all roughly the same size.

2. Spread the vegetables in a gratin dish or sauté pan in which they fit snugly. Add ½ cup of water; the water should coat the bottom of the pan. Dot the vegetables with butter or oil, sprinkle them with sugar, and season with salt and pepper. Bring the water to boiling, cover the pot, and cook the vegetables at a simmer for 20 to 30 minutes, until tender. The liquid should be reduced to a syrup; if more than that remains, remove the vegetables with a slotted spoon to a bowl and boil the liquid over high heat until it is syrupy. Put the vegetables back and reheat gently, stirring to coat them with the liquid. Taste for salt and pepper and serve sprinkled with parsley.

AHEAD OF TIME NOTE:

This can be made many hours in advance of serving. Reheat gently.

GRATED ZUCCHINI

1½ to 2 pounds zucchini
Salt

2 tablespoons olive oil

½ cup minced shallot

2 teaspoons minced garlic
Freshly ground black pepper

In August and September, we all look for imaginative ways to cook and enjoy zucchini and wish that, say, tomatoes were as easy to grow. Don't let their plenty discourage you from cooking and eating zucchini — try this.

1. With a hand grater or, a much easier method, the fine grater of a food processor or standing mixer, grate the zucchini.

2. Put the zucchini in a colander and sprinkle it with 2 tablespoons of salt. Let it stand for 20 to 25 minutes. Squeeze the zucchini dry in your hands and place it on two layers of paper towels, drying thoroughly.

3. Heat the oil in a heavy skillet or saucepan and sauté the shallot and garlic for about 5 minutes. Add the zucchini and cook, stirring, for about 7 to 8 eight minutes. Add pepper and taste for seasoning. Serve immediately or reheat later.

VARIATION:

Defrost a 10-ounce package of frozen spinach and squeeze it dry with your hands. If you're using fresh spinach, clean 1 pound, remove the tough stems, and with the water clinging to the leaves, cook it for about 2 minutes. Chop the spinach and add it to the zucchini after it has cooked for 5 minutes. Cook an additional 5 minutes, covered.

GREEN BEANS IN TOMATO SAUCE

In my childhood, green beans were ubiquitous — my mother, my friends' mothers, and all my aunts cooked green beans all the time in ways not worth recording. It was a revelation to encounter these Sephardic beans, equally good hot or cold, full of flavor, and still green!

1. Sauté the onion and garlic in the oil until soft.
2. Add the tomatoes and beans. Salt the beans and sprinkle with pepper. Cook for 15 to 20 minutes, adding a little water if necessary.
3. Sprinkle the beans with lemon juice and serve hot or at room temperature.

1 cup minced onion

2 tablespoons minced garlic

4 tablespoons olive oil

1 pound tomatoes, fresh or canned, peeled and chopped

2 pounds green beans, ends removed

Salt

Freshly ground black pepper

2 teaspoons lemon juice

IRANIAN SPINACH AND GREEN HERB PIE

2 pounds fresh spinach or 2
10-ounce packages frozen
spinach

1½ cups chopped parsley

¾ cup chopped dill

½ cup chopped scallion,
including some green
tops

1 tablespoon vegetable oil

¼ to ½ cup flour or matzo
meal

4 large eggs, lightly beaten
Salt
Freshly ground black
pepper

Letty Cottin Pogrebin is a writer and an excellent cook. She made this delicious pie at a dinner for a friend who had just returned from several months in Italy. What would our friend have missed during her time away? Jewish food! When I asked for the recipe, Letty told me it was from *The New York Times*, many years ago. This is my version of Letty's version of a recipe that appeared in a Passover article in *The New York Times*.

1. Preheat the oven to 350 degrees.

2. If using fresh spinach, wash it carefully and remove the thick stems. Dry and chop the spinach. If using frozen spinach, defrost it and squeeze out all the moisture.

3. Combine the spinach, parsley, dill, scallion, and vegetable oil in a bowl. Add ¼ cup flour or matzo meal and the eggs. With a wooden spoon, mix to combine. The mixture should be thick but slightly runny. Add salt and pepper and additional flour if necessary.

4. Spread the mixture in a 1- or 1½-quart baking dish. If the dish is shallow, bake the spinach for 25 to 30 minutes; if the dish is deep and the mixture is mounded, it might take as long as 40 minutes. The pie is done when it is completely set and coming away from the sides of the pan. It's best hot but can also be served at room temperature.

(JUST PLAIN) GREEN BEANS

Green beans can be thick and old, young and thin, or many sizes in between. This cooking technique yields great texture no matter the size. Buy perky beans; avoid the droopy discolored ones, even though picking them one by one becomes a bit of a chore. Make sure you use flavorful olive oil — a lot depends on it.

1 pound green beans
Salt
2 tablespoons olive oil or butter
Freshly ground black pepper

1. Bring a large quantity of salted water to boiling. Add the beans, sprinkle with salt (this helps set the color), and cook at a brisk boil until tender, from 5 to 10 minutes. Taste one to make sure the beans are done.

2. Drain. Put the pot back on the stove over low heat to evaporate the remaining water. Add the beans and toss to dry them.

3. Turn the beans into a serving dish, drizzle them with oil or butter, and season with salt and pepper.

LEEKS VINAIGRETTE

18 thin leeks (see Note)

4 tablespoons wine vinegar

1 tablespoon Dijon mustard

Salt

Freshly ground black pepper

4 tablespoons minced white of scallion or shallot

½ to ¾ cup olive oil

2 tablespoons minced parsley

Olive oil, a major component of this dish, is one of the first cooking oils — it was made in the Levant five thousand years ago. It was used to anoint Aaron and his sons as priests (Exodus 30:22: "The Lord spoke unto Moses, saying take choice spices...and olive oil. Make of this a sacred anointing oil") and also used to light the candelabra in the Temple.

This makes a good first course, or serve it instead of a lettuce salad. The better the olive oil, the better the dish.

1. Trim the leeks to a uniform size. Remove the tough green tops, leaving some tender greens. Wash the leeks under cold running water to remove all grit and dirt.

2. Bring 2 to 3 inches of salted water to boiling in a wide skillet. Place the leeks in the skillet and boil until tender, anywhere from 10 to 20 minutes.

3. Make the dressing while the leeks are cooking: Put the wine vinegar in a deep dish. Whisk in the mustard, salt, pepper, and scallion. Slowly beat in the olive oil (use more or less, depending on the amount of acidity you like). Alternatively, put all the ingredients (except the parsley) in a screw-top jar and shake to combine.

4. Drain the leeks on paper towels. Either add them to the dressing, spooning it over to cover the leeks, or place the leeks on a serving dish and pour the dressing over. Sprinkle with parsley and serve warm or at room temperature.

NOTE:

If you can't find thin leeks, use what you can find, adjusting the cooking time accordingly. It's best to use leeks of roughly the same diameter so they cook in the same amount of time.

AHEAD OF TIME NOTE:

You can make these several hours in advance of serving, but they're best when not refrigerated.

SUGAR SNAP PEAS AND CARROTS

The ubiquitous peas and carrots of my childhood weren't deemed cooked enough unless their color and texture were completely changed from their natural state. Sugar snaps are a relatively new hybrid whose pods are edible. They are delicious alone but make a lively color and texture contrast with the carrots. I love this contemporary (and delicious) version of an old-fashioned (and perhaps justifiably maligned) dish.

1. String the peas by snapping off the tip and pulling gently on the string down the concave side.

2. Peel the carrots and cut them into 1½- to 2-inch lengths; cut the lengths into halves, thirds, or quarters, depending on their thickness.

3. Bring a saucepan of water to boiling. Add 1 teaspoon of salt and the carrots. If they are fresh from the garden, don't bother with the sugar; older carrots, supermarket carrots sold in plastic bags, for example, will benefit from the sugar. Boil for 2 to 3 minutes, until the carrots are just tender. Drain. If using immediately, keep the carrots warm in a steamer over a small quantity of boiling water. If making in advance, cool them quickly under cold running water and set them aside, covered and refrigerated.

4. Just before serving, bring a pot of water to boiling. Add the peas and cook for 2 to 3 minutes. Drain them and toss with the warm carrots. If the carrots were cooked in advance, add them to the peas for the last minute.

5. Combine the butter and lemon juice and pour over the vegetables. Toss, season with salt and pepper, and serve. If you're using broth rather than butter, eliminate the lemon juice. Or, omit the butter and broth and season just with lemon juice, salt, and pepper.

1 pound sugar snap peas

1 pound carrots

Salt

2 teaspoons sugar

5 tablespoons hot melted butter or hot chicken broth

3 tablespoons lemon juice

Freshly ground black pepper

ROASTED ROOT VEGETABLES

4 tablespoons goose fat or olive oil

4 small turnips, peeled and quartered

2 parsnips, peeled, halved horizontally and then vertically sliced

4 carrots, scraped, halved horizontally and then vertically sliced

2 baking potatoes, peeled and thickly sliced

2 onions, coarsely chopped

Salt

Freshly ground black pepper

This dish is very flexible — if you have more parsnips, add them; if your family loves carrots, use more. The finished dish is indescribably wonderful made with the goose fat you carefully harbored and rendered (page 120) from the roast goose; it is good, too, with olive oil.

1. Preheat the oven to 450 degrees.

2. Melt the goose fat in, or add the olive oil to, a roasting pan large enough to hold all the vegetables in one layer.

3. Add the vegetables to the roasting pan. Add salt and pepper and mix well. Spread the vegetables in one layer and place the pan in the preheated oven for 1 hour, turning and tossing 2 or 3 times. Turn the vegetables into a decorative dish and serve.

ROOT VEGETABLE PUREE

This puree brightens a winter meal. It's good with fish or other dairy (or pareve) meals.

1. Peel and coarsely chop the vegetables. Place them in a saucepan and cover with cold salted water. Bring to boiling, lower the heat, and simmer for 20 minutes, until the vegetables are tender.

2. Drain the vegetables and puree them in a food processor with the milk. Return the vegetables to the saucepan and season with a pinch of cayenne, salt, and black pepper. Reheat, and serve sprinkled with parsley.

NOTE:

This is a forgiving dish; the proportions are flexible, as are the ingredients.

½ pound turnips

½ pound parsnips

½ pound potatoes

½ cup milk

Pinch cayenne

Salt

Freshly ground black pepper

¼ cup minced parsley

SAUTÉED MUSHROOMS

8 to 10 ounces fresh cultivated mushrooms

4 tablespoons olive oil

2 tablespoons minced garlic

½ cup minced parsley

½ cup fresh bread crumbs

Salt

Freshly ground black pepper

2 tablespoons lemon juice

The Russians are great mushroom hunters (see *Anna Karenina*). The Jews, outsiders in so many ways, shared this passion. This recipe requires no further hunting than your local supermarket.

1. Wipe the mushrooms with a damp paper towel, carefully removing dirt. Discard the stem tip and slice the mushrooms thickly; you should have about 4 cups.

2. Heat the oil in a large, heavy skillet. Toss the mushrooms in the oil over high heat for 5 to 10 minutes, depending on the size of the pan. If the mushrooms are crowded, this step will take longer. When the mushrooms' moisture has evaporated and they begin to color and fill the room with their aroma, add the garlic and parsley. Sauté for another 2 minutes. Add the bread crumbs and sauté for a few more minutes. Season with salt, pepper, and lemon juice, and serve.

SAUTÉED
SWISS CHARD

Swiss chard is a leafy green — it looks like overgrown spinach, though the taste is more assertive and the texture is meatier. Chard comes in both red and green. The ruby is stronger in flavor. You can combine the two or use one or the other alone.

2 pounds Swiss chard

2 tablespoons olive oil

1 cup minced onion

2 tablespoons grated orange peel

1. Soak the chard in lots of cold water, making sure all sand and grit is removed. Drain. Separate the leaves from the large red or pale green stems. If the chard is young, you needn't remove the stems. Remove any strings from mature leaves and slice the leaves into julienne strips. Chop about half the stems into ½-inch chunks, discarding the bottoms. If you use more than half the stems, the finished dish might be bitter.

2. Heat the oil in a large sauté pan and slowly cook the onion. When the onion softens, add the chard stems. Sauté for 10 to 15 minutes, until tender, stirring from time to time. Add the leaves and cover the pan to help reduce the volume quickly — like spinach, chard cooks down considerably. When it all fits in the pan, remove the cover and sauté for 2 to 3 minutes, until the leaves are soft and bright green. If there's a lot of liquid in the pan, raise the heat and stir for a few moments to evaporate the moisture. Stir in the orange peel and serve.

AHEAD OF TIME NOTE:
You can cook the chard several hours ahead of serving. Reheat over low heat and stir in the orange peel just before you serve.

SAUTÉED WILD MUSHROOMS

4 tablespoons vegetable oil

2 cups chopped onion

1 pound assorted "wild" mushrooms: cremini, portobello, shiitake

Salt

Freshly ground black pepper

¼ cup chopped parsley

This couldn't be easier to make; the hardest part is finding the wild mushrooms. This combination is not so wild, however, that you can't find it at your local greengrocer.

1. Wipe the mushrooms with damp paper towels, carefully removing dirt. Discard the stem tip and slice the mushrooms; you should have about 7 cups.

2. Heat the oil over medium heat in a 10-inch skillet or sauté pan. Sauté the onion until completely soft, about 15 minutes. Lower the heat to keep the onion from coloring.

3. Add the mushrooms. Stir to combine with the onion. Add salt and pepper. Sauté until the mushrooms are soft, 5 to 15 minutes, depending on the type of mushrooms. Sprinkle with parsley just before serving.

AHEAD OF TIME NOTE:

These can be made a few hours in advance of serving. Leave them in the sauté pan; don't refrigerate. Reheat just before serving.

SPICY SAUTÉED BROCCOLI

Broccoli is a versatile, widely available green vegetable. This quick-cooking dish adds a little spice to a plain meal.

1. Separate the florets from the broccoli stalks. Trim, peel, and slice the stalks. Cut the florets into ½-inch pieces.

2. Heat the oil in a skillet and add the garlic. Sauté over low heat for 6 to 7 minutes. Add the broccoli; sprinkle it with red-pepper flakes, salt, and pepper. Add ½ cup water, cover, and cook for 5 minutes. Uncover and cook until the water evaporates, about 2 to 3 minutes. Serve hot or at room temperature with lemon wedges.

3 pounds broccoli

4 tablespoons olive oil

3 tablespoons minced garlic

Crushed red-pepper flakes

Salt

Freshly ground black pepper

Lemon wedges

*Serves 2 or 3 as a main
course, 4 to 6 as
a first course*

4 large portobello
   mushrooms, about 1
   pound

3 tablespoons olive oil

1½ pounds fresh spinach

5 garlic cloves, peeled and
   sliced

¼ cup matzo meal or bread
   crumbs

   Salt

   Freshly ground black
   pepper

1 egg, lightly beaten

SPINACH-STUFFED PORTOBELLO MUSHROOMS

Portobellos are cultivated, full-grown cremini mushrooms. They have a nice meaty flavor, which, combined with their large size, makes them suitable as a main course. They are great for stuffing. Vegetarians and carnivores alike find this dish a satisfying main course. This is a good addition to a vegetarian Shabbat.

1. Preheat the oven to 400 degrees.

2. Snap the stems off the mushrooms and wipe them with a damp cloth. With the back of a small knife, gently scrape out and discard the gills. Brush the portobellos with some of the olive oil, both top and bottom. Place the mushrooms in a large skillet or other ovenproof pan and cook in the oven for about 10 minutes. Chop the stems, discarding their bottoms.

3. Stem and wash the spinach. Shake dry and chop.

4. Heat the remaining olive oil in a skillet. Sauté the garlic for 2 to 3 minutes, along with the mushroom stems. Add the spinach and cover the pan. Cook over low heat for 3 to 4 minutes. Remove the cover, raise the heat, and evaporate any liquid. Let cool. Add the matzo meal or bread crumbs, salt, pepper, and the egg. Mix well. Taste for seasoning.

5. Mound the spinach on the mushrooms. Place in the oven for 5 minutes, remove, and serve, or let cool and serve at room temperature.

AHEAD OF TIME NOTE:

This dish can be prepared ahead through most of step 4. After cooling the spinach, set it aside until you're ready to complete the dish. Just before its final cooking, add the matzo meal and the egg.

SWEET AND SOUR CABBAGE

Traditionally made with red cabbage, this is also delicious (and a pleasing pure white) with white cabbage.

In a large skillet, sauté the onion in the oil over medium heat. When the onion softens, add the cabbage and apples, cider vinegar, sugar, raisins, and 4 tablespoons of water. Mix well. Cover the skillet and cook over low heat for 30 to 40 minutes, until the cabbage is completely soft.

AHEAD OF TIME NOTE:

This dish is good hot or at room temperature and can be made in advance and reheated

2 cups sliced onion

3 tablespoons vegetable oil

8 to 10 cups shredded cabbage

4 tart apples, peeled, cored, and sliced (about 4 cups)

4 tablespoons cider vinegar

2 tablespoons sugar

4 to 6 tablespoons golden raisins

Vegetables

WARM CABBAGE SLAW

- 2 tablespoons olive oil
- 1 large red onion, peeled and thinly sliced
- 1 Savoy cabbage, cored and thinly sliced
- 2 tart apples, peeled, cored, and sliced
- ½ pound cultivated mushrooms, wiped clean and sliced
- Wine vinegar
- Salt
- Freshly ground black pepper

This is a surprise, as few people expect a tart, warm salad.

Heat the oil in a large sauté pan. Sauté the onion for about 5 minutes, until softened. Add the cabbage, apples, and mushrooms. Sauté for a few minutes, add a splash of wine vinegar, salt, and pepper. This is good hot from the skillet, at room temperature, or even cold.

SALADS

We remember...the cucumbers and melons,
and the leeks and the onions and the garlic.

NUMBERS 11: 5

NOT ALL SALADS ARE RAW, nor are they always lettuce or vegetables. Grains and pulses make delicious cold salads, and rice is the basis of a lavish cold main course. Sephardic and American, rather than Ashkenazic, salads are usually cold and provide a counterpoint of texture or temperature or both to a meal. Salad is particularly welcome at a lavish Shabbat meal, as its usually acidic dressing punctuates the otherwise heavy foods. Salads are also an excellent component of a vegetarian meal.

BEET AND GREEN BEAN SALAD

This colorful and delicious salad is good as an appetizer, served on lettuce leaves, or as an accompaniment to roasts.

1. Cut the beets into julienne strips.

2. Top and tail the beans. Place them in a large quantity of boiling water, salting them after the water returns to boiling. Simmer for 5 minutes. Drain the beans and spread them on paper towels to drain further and dry. Cut them into roughly 2-inch lengths.

3. In a large serving bowl, whisk the wine vinegar with the shallots, salt, pepper, and mustard. Slowly whisk in the olive oil.

4. Add the beets and beans to the dressing, tossing gently to coat.

5. Just before serving, add the walnuts and mix through. Push the egg through a sieve over the salad as a garnish.

1 pound beets (4 or 5 small), roasted and still warm (page 127)

1 pound green beans

2 tablespoons wine vinegar

3 tablespoons minced shallot

Salt

Freshly ground black pepper

1 tablespoon Dijon mustard

6 tablespoons olive oil

½ cup walnut pieces

1 hard-boiled egg (see Note, page 38), for garnish

BEET AND APPLE SALAD

2 pounds beets (8 to 10 small to medium), roasted and still warm (page 127)

1 tablespoon wine vinegar

1 cup walnut halves

2 tablespoons freshly squeezed lemon juice

5 tablespoons olive oil

Salt

Freshly ground black pepper

½ teaspoon Dijon mustard

1 cup minced onion

1 pound tart, crisp apples (Winesap, McIntosh, Granny Smith)

1. Slice the beets and combine them with the wine vinegar; let sit for 30 minutes.

2. Raise the temperature of the oven to 400 degrees. Spread the walnuts on a cookie sheet and toast them for 10 minutes. Watch carefully; they burn quickly.

3. Combine the lemon juice, olive oil, salt, pepper, and mustard in a serving bowl. Add the onion; stir to combine.

4. Quarter the apples, core, and peel. Slice each quarter thinly (you'll have about 3 cups); add to the onion mixture. Add the beets and walnuts; mix well.

AHEAD OF TIME NOTE:

This salad can be made early in the day. If you are making it just before serving, leave enough time for the beets to absorb the wine vinegar and for the onion to soften in the dressing. Don't add the walnuts until just before serving.

CARROT SALAD

Food processors or stand mixers with a grater attachment make this an easy preparation. It's colorful and tasty and is another welcome winter salad.

1. Scrape the carrots and chop them into chunks.

2. In the bowl in which you plan to serve the salad, whisk together the lemon juice, mustard, and salt. Whisk in the oil.

3. Using the large grating disk of a food processor or standing mixer, grate the carrots and onions. If you're using a standing mixer, you can grate the vegetables directly into the serving bowl.

4. Add pepper and the parsley; mix well and refrigerate the salad for an hour or so (or even a day or so — after that the salad loses its fresh taste) before serving.

12 medium carrots, about 1¼ pounds

2 tablespoons lemon juice

½ teaspoon Dijon mustard

Salt

4 tablespoons olive oil

2 onions, quartered

Freshly ground black pepper

6 tablespoons minced parsley

CHICKPEA SALAD

1 pound dried chickpeas (2 cups) or 2 15-ounce cans chickpeas, drained (see Note)

4 tablespoons freshly squeezed lemon juice

1 tablespoon salt

Freshly ground black pepper

2 garlic cloves, peeled and minced

1 teaspoon toasted cumin seeds, ground (see Note, page 123)

½ teaspoon cayenne

8 to 10 tablespoons olive oil

½ cup chopped pimento

½ cup chopped parsley

Versatile, delicious, and full of symbolism, chickpeas make a wonderful salad. Perhaps best known as the main ingredient in both felafel, the king of Israeli street food, and hummus, the ubiquitous sesame-paste-and-chickpea spread, chickpeas also make an appealing side salad. Serve this with couscous or roast chicken or plain broiled fish. It's also good as a first course, served on lettuce leaves and accompanied with olives, radishes, and cherry tomatoes.

1. Soak the chickpeas in cold water to cover for 3 to 4 hours or overnight. Alternatively, drain the canned chickpeas, wash them in a colander, and dry; skip step 2.

2. Cook the chickpeas, partially covered, in simmering water to cover for 1 to 1½ hours, until they are tender but not mushy. Drain.

3. While the chickpeas cook, make the dressing in a serving bowl. Beat the lemon juice with the salt, pepper, garlic, cumin, and cayenne. Slowly beat in the olive oil.

4. While the chickpeas are still warm, combine them with the dressing. Let sit for at least an hour.

5. Stir in the pimento and parsley just before serving.

NOTE:

I prefer dried chickpeas for this salad, because they are firmer and retain their texture.

COLESLAW

This is a good accompaniment to stews and cholents. These quantities make quite a lot of coleslaw, but it's good to have around for snacking and Shabbat meals. It's also a good party dish. The recipe can easily be halved.

1. Discard the limp outer leaves of the cabbages. Quarter and core the cabbages. Slice them by hand into julienne strips or put them through the slicing disk of a food processor after cutting them to fit the feed tube. Grate the carrots and onions.

2. In a large serving bowl, combine the mayonnaise, ketchup, vinegar, horseradish, salt, and pepper. Beat to combine.

3. Toss the vegetables with the dressing and serve.

AHEAD OF TIME NOTE:
The consistency of this salad changes as it sits: when just tossed it's quite crisp; as it sits, the slaw softens.

1 2- to 3-pound white cabbage

1 2- to 3-pound red cabbage

8 carrots

2 large onions

2 cups mayonnaise

1 cup ketchup

2 tablespoons white vinegar

2 tablespoons prepared white horseradish, drained

Salt

Freshly ground black pepper

COUSCOUS SALAD

1 cup couscous (not
  instant)

2 cups boiling water

Salt

Freshly ground black
pepper

2 tablespoons lemon juice

4 tablespoons olive oil

1 cup corn kernels, scraped
  from cobs or frozen

1 cup shelled peas, fresh or
  frozen

1 medium red pepper,
  diced

1 cup minced red onion

4 tablespoons minced
  parsley

Couscous is both a grain — tiny granules of semolina wheat —
and the name of a finished dish, a North African specialty (see
page 138). This Israeli salad is a wonderful accompaniment to
fish; it's also good with chicken.

1. Cover the couscous with the boiling water. Let sit for 5
   minutes or so, until the water is absorbed.

2. Place two inches of water in a saucepan into which a
   steamer will fit. Bring the water to boiling, fit in the
   steamer, add the couscous to the steamer, and cover the
   saucepan. Steam for 5 minutes. Remove the steamer by the
   ring at its top; keep the water simmering.

3. Transfer the couscous to a mixing bowl and fluff the grains
   with your fingers. Add salt, pepper, the lemon juice, and
   the olive oil. Mix well to combine.

4. To the simmering water, add the corn and peas. Cook for 2
   to 3 minutes. Drain them and add them to the couscous
   along with the red pepper, red onion, and parsley. Serve at
   room temperature. The salad will keep for a day or two,
   refrigerated. Bring it back to room temperature before
   serving.

VARIATION:

This salad is very adaptable: add green beans, briefly cooked, or
asparagus, cooked until tender and chopped. For a more sub-
stantial salad, add leftover chicken or meat and serve it for
lunch.

FATTOUSH

This pungent salad is known throughout the Middle East. Syrian Jews have brought it with them to America. It's a delicious, refreshing salad, particularly good in winter when salad ingredients are scarce.

1. Preheat the oven to 400 degrees.

2. Split the pitas open, cut them into wedges, and toss them with 3 tablespoons of the olive oil. Spread in one layer on a cookie sheet and toast in the oven until crisp, 15 to 20 minutes. Set aside.

3. In a mortar with a pestle, make a paste with the garlic clove and 1 teaspoon of salt; alternatively, mash the garlic through a garlic press and combine it with the salt in the salad bowl.

4. Peel, seed, and chop the cucumbers. Wash, stem, and chop the mint and parsley.

5. Beat the lemon juice in a salad bowl with the garlic paste. Slowly beat in the remaining olive oil. Add the cucumbers, mint, parsley, and scallions. Stir to combine. Just before serving, toss in the toasted pita.

2 pita breads
10 tablespoons olive oil
1 garlic clove, peeled
  Salt
3 medium cucumbers
½ cup mint leaves (see Note)
1 cup parsley
4 tablespoons lemon juice
1 cup chopped scallion, including some green tops

VARIATION:

This is a flexible salad. It always has cucumber, but you can add 1 chopped green pepper or 1 cup chopped celery or chopped hearts of romaine lettuce. In summer, when really ripe tomatoes are available, you can add one or two, chopped and seeded, to the salad. In winter, add halved cherry tomatoes.

NOTE:

If you can't find mint, increase the amount of parsley.

MOROCCAN SALADS

Little salads were served and constantly replenished throughout a Shabbat meal in Morocco, whose main item was frequently couscous (see page 138). Serve these with couscous or roast chicken or choucroute or breast of veal — or any main course at all.

CARROT SALAD

CARROT SALAD

- 2 bay leaves
- 5 parsley sprigs
- 1 pound carrots (8 to 10 medium)
- 4 tablespoons lemon juice
- 1 teaspoon toasted cumin seeds, ground (see Note, page 123)
- 1 teaspoon grated fresh ginger (see Note)
- 1 tablespoon grated onion (see Note)
- 2 garlic cloves, peeled
- 9 tablespoons olive oil
  Salt
  Freshly ground black pepper
- 2 tablespoons minced parsley

1. Bring 1 quart of water to boiling with the bay leaves and parsley sprigs.

2. Scrape the carrots and slice them into thin disks. Add the carrots to the boiling water. Off the heat, let them sit for 2 to 3 minutes. Drain, and dry the carrots on paper towels.

3. Measure the lemon juice into a serving dish. Whisk in the cumin, ginger, and onion; press the garlic cloves into the dressing mixture. Slowly whisk in the olive oil. Add the carrots and mix gently. Add salt and pepper, to taste. Refrigerate for at least 1 hour before serving, sprinkled with parsley.

NOTE:

To grate fresh ginger, peel a piece about the size of your thumb. Grate it over wax paper on the small holes of a box grater. To grate an onion, peel a small one and grate as for the ginger. Use the liquid, too.

TOMATO SALAD

TOMATO SALAD

- 5 or 6 tomatoes (or 8 plum tomatoes)
- 4 tablespoons minced parsley
- ¼ cup minced scallion
- ½ cup diced green pepper
- ½ cup diced celery
- 5 tablespoons olive oil
- 2 tablespoons lemon juice
  Salt
  Freshly ground black pepper

Peel the tomatoes with a swivel-bladed vegetable peeler. This is a trick of Marcella Hazan's, and it's a much simpler method than parboiling the tomato. Dice and seed the tomatoes. Place them in a serving bowl with the remaining ingredients. Mix and serve.

ORANGE AND OLIVE SALAD

1. In a serving bowl, combine the olive oil, lemon juice, garlic, cayenne, cumin, and parsley. Whisk to combine. Add the olives.

2. With a swivel-bladed vegetable peeler, remove the zest of one orange. Leave the white pith on the orange. Mince the zest and add it to the dressing. Peel what remains on the orange by slicing off the stem end and its opposite end. Stand the orange on a board and, following the curve of the fruit, slice off the skin with a very sharp paring knife. Repeat with the remaining oranges, without first removing the zest. You might take some orange flesh with the peel — that's okay. Capture any juice that's released and put it into the serving bowl. With a sharp knife, cutting between the membranes, remove the orange segments, again over the serving bowl to catch the juice. Put the orange segments in the serving bowl. Squeeze what remains of the orange in your hand into the serving bowl. Mix to combine all ingredients and serve. Or, cover and refrigerate for several hours before serving.

NOTE:

The Italians make a wonderful gadget that looks like a garlic press but is actually an olive pitter. If you can't find one, slice the olives in half and remove the pit. It's worth your sanity to leave a little olive flesh on the pit.

ORANGE AND
OLIVE SALAD

4 tablespoons olive oil

2 tablespoons lemon juice

1 tablespoon minced garlic

Pinch cayenne

1 teaspoon toasted cumin seeds, ground (see Note, page 123)

½ cup minced parsley

35 to 40 oil-cured black olives, pitted (see Note)

6 navel oranges

FENNEL AND APPLE SALAD

2 fennel bulbs (about 2 pounds)

2 tart apples

2 tablespoons lemon juice

1 tablespoon olive oil

Salt

Freshly ground black pepper

⅓ cup toasted almonds

Fennel fronds

Fennel is a fall and winter vegetable, undervalued, I think, in this country. The stalks can be dried and used as a bed for roasting chicken or fish. Save the feathery fronds for decoration. For this recipe, use the youngest fennel you can find.

1. Trim the fennel bulbs of their stalks and thinly slice each bulb. Reserve the feathery fronds for decoration.

2. Peel, core, and slice the apples.

3. In a salad bowl or shallow serving dish, whisk together the lemon juice, olive oil, salt, and pepper. Add the fennel and apples; toss the salad with the almonds, scatter the fronds over the salad, and serve.

ORZO SALAD

This rice-shaped pasta is very versatile. It can be served as a salad or dropped into soup, as the Italians do — it is one of the pastina in *pastina in brodo*. Serve the salad as a first course, on lettuce leaves, or as an accompaniment to roasts.

½ pound (1¼ cups) orzo
1 tablespoon olive oil
Salt
Freshly ground black pepper
1 red pepper
½ cup mayonnaise
1 tablespoon Dijon mustard
½ cup minced scallion
½ cup toasted walnuts
Boston lettuce leaves

1. Cook the orzo in a large quantity of boiling, salted water, 8 to 10 minutes. The orzo should be soft but still slightly firm. Drain it and put it in a serving bowl with the olive oil. Season with salt and pepper and let cool.

2. Place the red pepper on a metal mesh screen (sold as splatter guards in hardware stores) over a gas flame to remove the skin. Alternatively, hold it over the flame with a skewer. Turn the pepper on all sides to char it. Let it cool and then peel and dice it (one pepper will yield about ½ cup). You can also peel the pepper with a swivel-bladed vegetable peeler. This method will give the salad a crunchier texture.

3. Combine the mayonnaise and mustard. Toss with the orzo along with the scallion and walnuts. Serve on lettuce leaves.

VARIATIONS:
You can add a cup of chopped leftover cooked chicken or meat and turn this into a main-course salad.

CELERY ROOT AND POTATO SALAD

1 pound all-purpose potatoes

1½ tablespoons wine vinegar

½ cup mayonnaise

1 tablespoon lemon juice

1 teaspoon Dijon mustard

1 pound celery root

½ cup minced parsley

I love celery root (also known as celeriac and celery knob). It has a crunch when raw and a bite when cooked that's irresistible. It pays to remember it when everyone is tired of cabbage and beets.

1. Peel and cube the potatoes. Cover them with cold water, bring to boiling, and simmer for 10 minutes or so, until the potatoes are tender. Drain.

2. Combine the potatoes with the wine vinegar and let them sit for about an hour; they should cool and absorb the vinegar.

3. Combine the mayonnaise, lemon juice, and mustard in a serving bowl.

4. Peel the celery root and chop it into pieces small enough to fit into the feed tube of a food processor or other grating mechanism. Grate the celery root and add it to the serving bowl with the dressing. Mix well. Let sit for about an hour.

5. Add the potatoes to the celery root, mix well, sprinkle with parsley, and serve.

RICE SALAD

This wonderful make-ahead dish is served by Italian Jews on Shabbat. It's excellent for shalosh seudot or lunch if "hot" and "covered" are not requirements in your household.

1. Cook the rice in a large quantity of boiling water for 12 minutes. Drain.

2. While the rice is still warm, stir in the white or wine vinegar, olive oil, salt, pepper, and onion. Let cool to room temperature.

3. Cook the peas for 2 minutes in simmering water. Drain.

4. Add all the remaining ingredients to the rice, except the tomatoes, stirring to combine well. Garnish with the tomatoes before serving.

VARIATION:

You can add a lot to this salad: minced red pepper, 4 ounces of chopped anchovy fillets, and a dozen or so pitted black olives. You can also combine cooked dried or drained canned chickpeas with the rice, using a cup of each. Substitute 2 cups of chopped cooked chicken for the tuna, adding 1 teaspoon of dried tarragon to the warm rice with the vinegar and oil.

2 cups uncooked white rice

3 tablespoons distilled white vinegar or white-wine vinegar

6 tablespoons olive oil
Salt
Freshly ground black pepper

½ cup minced onion

1 cup shelled green peas, fresh or frozen

1 6-ounce can tuna, preferably packed in oil

¾ cup artichoke hearts, preserved in oil, drained and chopped

2 tablespoons capers, rinsed, drained, and dried

½ cup chopped parsley
Cherry tomatoes for garnish

RUSSIAN SALAD

1 pound beets

2 pounds potatoes

1 cup cubed carrot

1 cup shelled peas, fresh or frozen

½ cup mayonnaise

1 teaspoon dry mustard

2 teaspoons white-wine vinegar

2 tablespoons olive oil

1 cup minced scallion, including 2 inches of green top

1½ cups cubed, seeded cucumbers (2 medium cucumbers)

2 hard-boiled eggs (see Note, page 38), peeled and sliced

2 tablespoons capers, rinsed and dried

¼ cup minced dill

In her book *The Winter Vegetarian*, Darra Goldstein tells us that this delicious mixed vegetable salad was known in Russia as Olivier Salad, after an acclaimed nineteenth-century French chef who cooked in Moscow, or Capital Salad, frequently served as a first course in Soviet-era restaurants. In Italy it is Insalata Russa, once a Shabbat favorite; in France it's Salade Russe. Perhaps it traveled to those countries with immigrating Jews. I never ate a Russian Salad in Russia that was worth recording, but in its international variations, the salad's potential is obvious. The vegetables and their quantities given here should serve simply as a guide, because their type and quantity are flexible. The success of the salad depends largely on the proper cooking of the vegetables: the taste and texture contrasts are most appealing.

Serve the salad as an accompaniment to roast chicken or meat or as a first course, served on a bed of lettuce. It's quite filling, and with cold chicken or Gravlax (page 77) it's a satisfying lunch.

1. Preheat the oven to 400 degrees.

2. Cut off the beet greens, leaving about ½ inch of stems. Wash the beets carefully, taking care not to pierce them. Place the beets in a flat roasting pan with a little water, cover with foil, and roast for 45 to 90 minutes, depending on their age and size. The beets should be thoroughly tender; undercooked beets are bitter. Let the beets cool before peeling — if you shave off the stem, the skin will slip right off. Cut the beets into small dice; you should have about 2 cups.

3. Boil the potatoes until just tender. Cool, peel, and dice them in roughly the same size pieces as the beets.

4. Boil the carrot in salted water for 5 minutes, adding the peas for the last 15 seconds. Drain.

5. In a small bowl, whisk together the mayonnaise, mustard, wine vinegar, olive oil, and scallion.

6. Put the beets, potatoes, carrot, peas, and cucumbers in a large serving bowl — it looks especially nice in glass. Mix the dressing in thoroughly with the vegetables. Cover and refrigerate for at least 1 hour before serving, garnished with the hard-boiled eggs, capers, and dill.

AHEAD OF TIME NOTE:

The salad can be made a day in advance of serving, but the longer it sits, the less distinct the tastes and textures become; in addition, the cucumbers tend to waterlog the salad.

VARIATIONS:

The salad happily accommodates parboiled green beans, broccoli, and cauliflower. The Italians garnish it with anchovies, and the Russians put in a little chopped dill pickle, which adds a nice piquancy. Don't worry about authenticity — experiment.

DESSERTS

*Honey and sweet food
enlighten the eyes of man.*

TALMUD

PERHAPS THE JEWISH HOUSEWIFE was too overwhelmed with Shabbat preparations to find time to make elaborate desserts. The restrictions of kashrut limited her choices but not her imagination, which she often displayed with remarkable baking: strudel, rugelach, cakes — but rarely for Shabbat.

Because most Shabbat meals contain meat, the desserts in this chapter are pareve and take advantage of the fruits available here in the New World. Almost all should be made in advance. Some of these desserts are more familiar to kosher Jews than others; some, like Chiffon Cake, are pareve without seeming particularly Jewish. Many have the festive quality appropriate for Friday night; others are just right after a large meal.

APPLE-HONEY BROWN BETTY

This pareve apple dessert is a fall treat. Use the tartest, firmest apples you can find — Macouns are wonderful.

With a nonmeat meal, serve with ice cream or whipped cream.

½ cup vegetable oil

2 pounds tart apples

4 tablespoons brown sugar

3 tablespoons lemon juice

1½ tablespoons grated lemon peel (see Note)

½ teaspoon ground cinnamon

1 cup whole-wheat flour

½ cup honey

1. Preheat the oven to 350 degrees.

2. Use some of the oil to grease a 1-quart baking dish, 9 to 10 inches in diameter.

3. Quarter, core, peel, and slice the apples; you should have about 5 cups.

4. Combine the brown sugar, lemon juice, lemon peel, and cinnamon in a bowl. Add the apple slices, mixing well.

5. Pile the apples into the baking dish.

6. Heat the remaining oil. Stir in the flour and honey, mashing out any lumps. With a thin metal spatula, spread this over the apples. Place in the oven and bake for 30 minutes. Serve warm or at room temperature.

NOTE:

To grate citrus peel, you can run the fruit against a box grater, or, as I do, you can remove the peel (leaving the bitter white pith behind) with a vegetable peeler. Then, either mince it with a sharp knife or pulse it in a miniprocessor or electric spice or coffee grinder.

APRICOT
COMPOTE

1 pound dried apricots

¼ cup sugar

1 tablespoon orange-flower
   water

¼ cup chopped almonds or
   pistachios

This is a popular Shabbat dessert in the Sephardic community of Brooklyn. The aromatic orange-flower water gives this simple dish a lot of distinction.

Cover the apricots with water (about 3 cups) and bring to boiling. Simmer until the apricots are plump and tender, 20 to 30 minutes. Remove the apricots with a slotted spoon. Add sugar to the liquid — ¼ cup, more or less — and bring to boiling to dissolve the sugar. Pour the syrup over the apricots, cool, and chill well. Before serving, add the orange-flower water and garnish with the chopped nuts.

BAKED APPLES

I love baked apples: they are homey and tasty and satisfying; maybe best of all, these are pareve. If there's no meat in your meal and no guilt in your life, serve them with heavy cream.

1. Preheat the oven to 350 degrees.

2. Core the apples with a grapefruit knife. Saw down gently, because you want to remove the entire core but leave the apple whole; don't penetrate the bottom. Once the apple is cored, with a vegetable peeler remove the skin from the top third of each apple.

3. Combine the raisins, almonds, and 6 tablespoons of the honey. Fill the apple cavities with the mixture. Stand the apples in an ovenproof dish in which they fit snugly. Pour ½ cup water into the bottom of the pan, along with the remaining tablespoon of honey.

4. Combine the sugar and cinnamon and sprinkle it over the apples. Place the apples in the preheated oven and bake for 30 to 45 minutes, basting with the pan liquid every 10 minutes. Cooking times will vary according to the size, type, and texture of the apples. They should be soft but not falling apart. Serve at room temperature, with their syrup poured over.

VARIATIONS:

Baked apples offer a real opportunity to be creative. Here are some of my favorite fillings: 1 tablespoon ginger preserves for each apple; if you have compote lingering in your fridge (it keeps for much longer than it remains interesting to the family), mince it and stuff about 1 or 1½ tablespoons into each apple; drizzle a little maple syrup into each apple.

6 Red or Golden Delicious apples

6 tablespoons raisins

6 tablespoons slivered toasted almonds

7 tablespoons honey

1 tablespoon sugar

¼ teaspoon cinnamon

Desserts

BANANA SORBET

4 overripe bananas
½ cup cold water
½ cup sugar
3 tablespoons
   fresh lemon juice

This is a good way to use bananas that are too ripe to slice into your morning cereal or will only rot over the weekend. This easy, delicious dessert is pareve. It's only drawback is also one of its assets — it must be made in advance. The actual work, however, takes only 5 minutes.

1. Peel and slice the bananas. Puree them with the water in a food processor or blender until smooth. Add the sugar and lemon juice and process just to combine. Pour the mixture into a bowl and refrigerate for a minimum of 3 hours and up to 3 days.

2. Whisk the mixture and pour it into the canister of an ice-cream maker. Follow the manufacturer's instructions for freezing. When the sorbet is thick, transfer it to a serving dish if you are eating right away or pack it into a plastic container for freezer storage. Place the sorbet in the refrigerator for 10 to 15 minutes before serving.

CHOCOLATE MERINGUES

These go well with fruit salad or compote; they are good for Shabbat and for Passover; they're also enjoyable with a cup of afternoon tea.

Vegetable oil

Flour or matzo cake meal

4 large egg whites

⅛ teaspoon cream of tartar

1 cup sugar

½ pound semisweet chocolate bits

1. Preheat the oven to 250 degrees. Line two baking sheets with parchment paper or aluminum foil. Lightly grease the aluminum foil lining and dust with flour or matzo cake meal; the parchment needs no preparation.

2. Beat the egg whites with the cream of tartar until almost stiff. Gradually add the sugar, beating until the whites are shiny and stiff.

3. Quickly fold in the chocolate bits.

4. Form the cookies with a tablespoon, mounding the batter onto the baking sheets about 2 inches apart.

5. Bake the meringues for about an hour, until they are firm and dry. After 30 minutes, switch the cookie sheets, back to front and top to bottom.

6. Cool the meringues on a rack and store airtight for up to 1 week. You can recrisp the meringues, if necessary, in a 200-degree oven.

CHIFFON CAKE

2¼ cups sifted cake flour

1 tablespoon baking powder

½ teaspoon salt

1½ cups superfine sugar

7 eggs

½ cup corn oil or safflower oil

2 teaspoons vanilla extract

2 teaspoons grated lemon zest

¼ teaspoon cream of tartar

Confectioners' sugar

Chiffon cake was "invented" in the late 1920s by a California insurance agent and hobby cook named Harry Baker. He sold the "formula" to General Mills in 1947, and it turned out the "secret" ingredient was vegetable oil. Chiffon cakes are popular with kosher cooks because they are pareve.

1. Preheat the oven to 325 degrees and position a rack in the lower third. Have a 10-inch tube pan ready, ungreased.

2. Sift together the flour, baking powder, salt, and ½ cup of the sugar. Set aside.

3. Separate 6 of the eggs. Place the yolks and the remaining whole egg in the bowl of a standing electric mixer. Beat for a few minutes and, a couple of tablespoons at a time, add ½ cup of sugar. In 3 to 4 minutes the mixture will be pale yellow and substantially thickened.

4. Pour in the oil in a steady stream. Add the vanilla extract and the lemon zest.

5. With the mixer speed at medium-low, add the dry ingredients to the yolks alternately with ¾ cup of water. If you're using a heavy-duty standing mixer, turn it off when you add the dry ingredients to prevent the flour from splattering all over the kitchen.

6. With clean beaters and bowl, whip the 6 egg whites on medium speed until frothy. Add the cream of tartar and beat until the whites form a soft shape. Add the remaining ½ cup of sugar, 1 or 2 tablespoons at a time. Beat until the whites are satiny and firm.

7. With a rubber spatula, fold ¼ of the yolk mixture into the whites. Gently scoop the whites over the remaining yolk mixture and quickly and thoroughly fold.

8. Carefully pour the batter into the pan. Center it on the rack and bake for 60 to 70 minutes, until the cake is golden and springs back to your touch.

9. Remove the cake from the oven and immediately invert the pan onto a cake rack. Let the cake cool completely. To remove the cake from the pan, set it upright and run a sharp

knife around the side of the pan and the center tube. Holding the tube, remove the outer rim from the cake. Slide the knife between the pan bottom and the cake to release it. Invert the cake onto a cake plate and remove the tube. Transfer the cake to a platter. Sprinkle the cake with confectioners' sugar if serving immediately. The cake will keep, well wrapped at room temperature, for 4 or 5 days.

VARIATIONS:

CHOCOLATE-NUT CHIFFON CAKE:
Omit the lemon zest and vanilla extract. Add 5 ounces of chopped semisweet chocolate and 1 cup of chopped walnuts to the batter, stirring to combine, before you add the egg whites.

ORANGE CHIFFON CAKE:
Omit the vanilla extract and lemon zest. Add 3 tablespoons of grated orange zest and substitute orange juice for all or some of the ¾ cup of water.

BUTTERSCOTCH CHIFFON CAKE:
Substitute 2 cups of brown sugar for the superfine sugar, adding it to the dry ingredients. Omit the lemon zest.

COFFEE SORBET

½ pound finely ground (as for espresso) coffee beans

½ cup plus 6 tablespoons sugar

1 quart boiling water

2 egg whites

Rum or brandy (optional)

This milkless coffee sorbet is refreshing after a meat meal. Serve it with Mandlebrot (page 250) or Chocolate Meringues (page 237).

1. Combine the ground coffee and ½ cup sugar in a metal bowl. Stir. Add the boiling water, whisking to dissolve lumps. Let the coffee mixture stand for 10 minutes. Refrigerate it until cold, at least 3 hours.

2. Strain the coffee mixture into another metal bowl through a strainer lined with cheesecloth or pour it through a coffee filter — you don't want any coffee grounds in the sorbet. Freeze the mixture in the bowl.

3. When the coffee mixture is almost set, beat the egg whites until stiff with the remaining 6 tablespoons of sugar. Fold the beaten whites into the icy coffee. Process for 15 to 20 minutes in an ice-cream machine. Serve the sorbet immediately or transfer it to a plastic container and freeze. Serve with a spoonful of rum or brandy if you wish.

DESSERT COUSCOUS

Couscous, tiny grains of semolina, is a North African staple. Here it is imaginatively used for dessert.

1 cup couscous

6 tablespoons margarine or butter

1 cup raisins

½ cup chopped dried dates

1 cup chopped dried apricots

3 tablespoons sugar

¼ teaspoon grated nutmeg

½ teaspoon ground cinnamon

1 cup apple juice

¼ cup slivered almonds, toasted

1. Add the couscous to 2 cups of boiling water. Let it stand; in about 5 minutes the grain will have absorbed the liquid.

2. Heat the margarine or butter in a saucepan that has a tight-fitting lid and is large enough to accommodate a steamer. Stir in the raisins, dates, apricots, sugar, a few gratings of nutmeg, and the cinnamon. Sauté for 5 minutes.

3. Add the apple juice to the dried fruits. Put a steamer basket in the saucepan over the dried fruits. Add the couscous to the steamer and cover the saucepan. Cook over low heat for 10 minutes.

4. Combine the couscous and the dried fruits in a serving bowl; stir in the almonds. Serve warm or at room temperature.

DRIED FRUIT COMPOTE

5 pounds mixed dried prunes, apricots, apples, pears

2 cups dry white wine

1 cup sugar

1 lemon, quartered

1 cinnamon stick

Lemon juice

Eastern Europeans relied on dried fruit, as fresh was rare in the cold climates of Poland and Russia. It's unlikely they knew apricots at all, so this is a New World compote. This traditional dish keeps for months and is delicious as is or served with ice cream or sherbet.

1. In a large saucepan, combine all the ingredients except the lemon juice with 2 cups of water. Bring the mixture to boiling, lower the heat, cover the pan, and simmer very slowly for 30 to 45 minutes, until the fruit is tender.

2. Remove the fruit from the heat and let it cool. Taste for seasoning — the compote may need more sugar or some lemon juice. Stored refrigerated in a covered jar, the compote will keep for a long time.

FRESH FRUIT
SALAD

Fruit salad is welcome, and pareve, in summer and winter. Always available are oranges, grapefruits, bananas, and apples. Use 3 oranges, peeled and segmented; 2 grapefruit, peeled and segmented; 2 tart, firm apples, quartered, peeled, cored and sliced; and 1 banana, peeled and sliced. Add 2 to 3 tablespoons of lemon juice and ¼ cup of honey. In winter, add ripe pears and seedless grapes. In summer, start with berries and add peaches, apricots, melon, plums. You can vary the taste by omitting the honey and adding ⅓ cup of sparkling wine or orange liqueur. Taste and add sugar, if necessary. Vary and experiment with different fruits — it's a wonderful dessert that's a bit of a tzimmes to make (lots of chopping, dicing, peeling) but requires no pots and no special technique. The salad is best the day you make it, though it should be refrigerated for 2 to 3 hours before you serve it.

GINGER-LEMON SORBET

5 cups water

2 cups sugar

½ cup coarsely chopped
peeled fresh ginger

2 tablespoons finely grated
lemon peel (see Note,
page 233)

½ cup freshly squeezed
lemon juice

This is an easy dessert to make and you don't need any special equipment. It's refreshing and unusual.

1. Combine the water, sugar, and ginger in a saucepan. Bring it to boiling, reduce the heat, and simmer for 15 minutes. Strain, discarding the ginger.

2. Return the liquid to the saucepan with the lemon peel. Bring to boiling and simmer for 3 minutes. Stir in the lemon juice and let the mixture cool.

3. Pour the liquid into a shallow 2½- to 3-quart (12 or 13 by 9 by 2–inch) glass or porcelain dish. Cover the liquid and freeze it until firm, at least 6 hours.

4. Dislodge the mixture with a table knife or spatula. Break up the sorbet and spoon it into the workbowl of a food processor to puree. Start with a small amount, adding more as the mixture purees. Return the sorbet to the dish, smooth it with a rubber spatula, and refreeze it until solid, at least 4 hours. The sorbet will keep for about 3 days; after that it loses its fresh taste. Let it soften in the refrigerator for 30 minutes before serving.

GRANNY SMITH SORBET

In my profession as a cookbook editor, I work with many talented cooks and cooking teachers, none more gifted and accessible than Marcella Hazan. When she and her husband and collaborator, Victor, came to a recipe-testing dinner, Marcella suggested I include this recipe. It appeared in *Marcella Cucina* and it's delicious.

1. Peel, core, and dice the apples.

2. Put the honey and sugar and 1 cup of water in a small saucepan and bring it to simmering over low heat. Cook the liquid down to a syrup half its original volume.

3. Puree the syrup, the apples, and all the remaining ingredients, including the grappa, if used, in a food processor.

4. Freeze the sorbet in an ice-cream maker and serve it when done or repack it in plastic and store it in the freezer.

3 Granny Smith apples

1 tablespoon honey

1 cup sugar

6 tablespoons freshly squeezed lemon juice

1 cup muscat wine, Asti Spumante, a California moscato, or other not-too-intensely sweet white wine

2 tablespoons grappa (optional)

GRAPEFRUIT AND WINE MOUSSE

1 cup grapefruit juice

1 cup dry white wine

¾ cup sugar

4 eggs, separated

2 tablespoons cornstarch

Mint leaves

This refreshing combination is a welcome one after a multi-course Shabbat meal. The mousse is light, with a nice taste kick. Make it in the morning for the evening meal.

1. In a saucepan, combine the grapefruit juice, wine, ½ cup of the sugar, the egg yolks, and the cornstarch. Heat, but don't boil, stirring constantly. When the mixture is thick enough to coat a metal spoon thickly, take it off the heat and let it cool.

2. Beat the egg whites with the remaining ¼ cup of sugar until stiff. Fold them into the cooled grapefruit mixture. Turn the mousse into stemmed glasses or a large bowl and refrigerate for several hours. Garnish with mint.

AHEAD OF TIME NOTE:

This keeps well for 12 hours; after that it separates. Give it a stir, and the taste will still be pleasing but the texture will no longer be mousselike.

GREENMARKET APPLESAUCE

This is the easiest, most delicious, most forgiving recipe I know. It is darn near perfect as is, but it also welcomes endless variations. I live near the Union Square Greenmarket in Manhattan, and the wide and wonderful variety of apples available there in autumn makes me miss just a little less the bounty of summer. If you can buy only one or two varieties, you may want to make one of the variations. This applesauce is delicious as a dessert, with a plain cake or cookies, or as an accompaniment to brisket and latkes, as a condiment.

3 pounds apples: McIntosh, Macoun, Jonathan, Winesap, Cortland, Northern Spy, Ida Red

1. Wash the apples and quarter them. Don't peel; don't core.

2. Place the apples in a wide, heavy pot with a lid; don't add any liquid. Turn the heat to very low, cover, and cook for 30 to 60 minutes, stirring from time to time. The timing will depend on the size of the apples and the size of the pan — apples in a shallow, wide skillet will cook faster than those cooked in a deep, narrow saucepan.

3. When the apples are completely cooked and mash easily with a wooden spoon, put them through a food mill. Voilà — applesauce that carries the rich taste of apples.

VARIATIONS:

Cook the apples with large strips of lemon peel. After pureeing, add ¼ to ½ cup of sugar, ⅛ to ½ teaspoon of cinnamon, a few grindings of nutmeg, and maybe ½ teaspoon of vanilla extract. You can also flavor the puree with ¼ to ½ cup of honey or maple syrup. Try these alone or in combinations that appeal to you.

JELLYROLL

1 tablespoon margarine

½ cup sifted cake flour

¼ cup sifted cornstarch

5 large eggs

Salt

½ cup sugar

1 teaspoon vanilla extract

Confectioners' sugar

1 cup jam, jelly, or fruit preserves

Jellyroll is a sponge cake baked in a large flat pan, spread with a filling, usually jelly, and rolled. It's fun to make, it looks good, and it's pareve. The better the filling, the better the finished jellyroll — so don't stint.

1. Preheat the oven to 350 degrees. Spread some of the margarine on the bottom and sides of a jellyroll pan, 15 × 10 × 1 inch deep; line with wax paper and grease that with margarine; dust with flour and set aside.

2. Sift the cake flour and cornstarch together into a mixing bowl.

3. Separate the eggs, placing the whites and yolks in separate bowls that will fit your standing mixer or are deep enough for your hand beater.

4. Add a pinch of salt to the egg whites and beat them until foamy. Gradually add 6 tablespoons of the sugar. Beat until the whites are satiny and firm but not dry.

5. With the same beaters, whisk the yolks with the remaining sugar. When thick and significantly lighter in color, add the vanilla extract. Keep beating until the batter falls back on itself in a ribbon — this will take 3 to 5 minutes, depending on your mixer.

6. Fold one-quarter of the whites into the yolk mixture. Put the flour mixture in a fine strainer and shake it over the yolk-whites mixture, tapping the side of the strainer as you do this. Fold in gently. When the dry ingredients are incorporated, gently fold in the remaining whites. The batter should be light, so work carefully and quickly.

7. Spread the batter in the prepared pan, smoothing the top with a metal spatula. Bake for 10 to 13 minutes; the top should be light golden and a toothpick inserted in the center should come out clean and dry.

8. While the cake bakes, dust a clean cotton or linen kitchen towel with confectioners' sugar in roughly the dimensions of the pan. As soon as the cake is done, invert the pan over the towel. Peel off the pan and the paper, using the testing toothpick, with a light touch, to give you a little leverage. With a sharp knife, cut away any crisp edges (this makes rolling easier). Roll the cake from one of the short edges, rolling the towel with it and using the towel as a guide. Set it on a rack to cool.

9. When the cake is cool, unroll it — it will retain a bit of its rolled shape. Spread the roll with the jam, jelly, or preserves — whichever you have chosen. Reroll the cake without the towel and place it on serving a plate, seam side down. Place 2 tablespoons of confectioners' sugar in a small sieve and shake it all over the top of the jellyroll.

NOTE:

The filled jellyroll will keep for a couple of days, well wrapped and refrigerated. The unfilled cake will keep, rolled in its cloth, for several hours, or overnight.

VARIATIONS:

SPICE JELLYROLL:

For the vanilla extract, substitute 1 teaspoon of cinnamon, ½ teaspoon of ground cloves, and ½ teaspoon of grated nutmeg; combine and add to the flour-cornstarch mixture.

NUT ROLL:

Add 1 cup of finely ground toasted almonds or hazelnuts to the batter in step 6.

MANDLEBROT

3 cups unbleached flour

1 tablespoon baking
  powder

¼ teaspoon salt

4 eggs

1 cup sugar

½ cup vegetable oil

½ teaspoon almond extract

½ teaspoon vanilla extract

1 tablespoon grated lemon
  zest

1½ cups slivered almonds

Mandlebrot, which means "almond bread" in Yiddish, is the Jewish version of Italian biscotti, or perhaps it's the other way around. My mother always served mandlebrot with tea after Shabbat dinner. The adults always had tea and they always dunked their mandlebrot in it. In Italy, they dunk biscotti in sweet wine.

1. Preheat the oven to 350 degrees. Lightly grease 2 cookie sheets.

2. Sift together the flour, baking powder, and salt.

3. Beat the eggs with the sugar until the mixture is thick and pale. Add the oil, extracts, and lemon zest. Beat to combine. Fold in the almonds. Stir in the flour mixture.

4. With moistened hands, shape the dough into 4 logs, about 2 inches in diameter. If the dough is too tacky to handle, add a little more flour. Place the logs on the prepared cookie sheets. Bake for 30 to 45 minutes, until lightly browned but still soft. Halfway through the baking, switch the cookie sheets front to back and top to bottom.

5. With a long, flat metal spatula, transfer the logs to a board and let them stand until you can handle them. If any dough sticks to the cookie sheet, scrape it off and re-oil the cookie sheet.

6. On the diagonal, cut each log into ½-inch slices; place the slices back on the cookie sheets. Bake 7 to 10 minutes per side, until the mandlebrot are lightly browned. Cool on a rack and store in an airtight container. They'll keep for about 2 weeks.

MEDITERRANEAN COMPOTE

The orange juice and dates reveal the origin of this compote: the Mediterranean rather than eastern Europe. It's fresh and lovely.

Put all the ingredients in a saucepan. Stir to combine and cook over low heat, partially covered, for 20 to 30 minutes. Let the compote cool and turn it into a serving dish. The compote will keep, refrigerated, for several weeks.

NOTE:

For this dish, I wash the orange, preferably a large navel, and remove the zest in long strips with a vegetable peeler. I then mince the strips. You can also chop the strips in a miniprocessor, though if you calculate the time it takes to find it and wash it after use, you're probably better off doing this chore on a board with a sharp knife.

½ pound pitted prunes
½ pound pitted dried dates
½ pound dried apricots
½ cup brewed tea
1 cup freshly squeezed orange juice
3 tablespoons minced orange zest (see Note)
Pinch cinnamon
1 tablespoon honey

MERINGUE SHELLS

4 egg whites (see Note)
Salt
⅛ teaspoon cream of tartar
1 cup sugar
½ teaspoon vanilla extract

These meringue shells are wonderful for serving fruit. They dress up rhubarb (page 256), strawberries, fruit salad. This recipe offers a lot of flexibility: you can make the cups as large as you like, or you can make two eight-inch shells or one ten-inch shell from this quantity.

1. Preheat the oven to 200 to 225 degrees. Line two cookie sheets with parchment paper or oil them lightly. Lightly trace eight to ten 4-inch circles on the parchment; or trace one 10-inch circle or two 8-inch circles, depending on how you want to use the shells.

2. Put the egg whites in the scrupulously clean mixing bowl of a standing mixer fitted with the whisk. Start beating on low speed, for just 1 or 2 minutes. Add a pinch of salt and the cream of tartar, raise the speed to medium, and beat until the whites barely hold a shape. Start beating in the sugar, in a slow steady stream, stopping from time to time to let the whites absorb it. When all the sugar is added, continue beating on high speed for 5 to 6 minutes, adding the vanilla. The whites will be glossy and stiff and the sugar absorbed. If the whites feel or taste grainy, keep beating.

3. Put the meringue in a pastry bag fitted with a 6-inch tip. Drop about 2 tablespoons of meringue into the center of each 4-inch circle, 4 into larger circles. Smooth out the meringue with a metal spatula to the edge of the traced circles. This will be the bottom of the shells. Create the edge by squeezing meringue from the bag to build a border at the edge of the circles. Two or three layers with the pasty bag will do it. Once you become skilled with a pastry bag (and it won't take long), use star tips and vary the tip size for different thicknesses and results.

4. Bake in the oven for 1 to 1½ hours. The meringues should stiffen and take on only a little color. Let the meringues sit for a few moments before running a sharp knife under the shells to loosen them from the paper. Be careful not to break them. Place the meringues on a rack until completely cool. They will keep well in an airtight container for about a week. Each 4-inch shell will hold 2 to 3 tablespoons of filling.

NOTE:

Eggs whites are easiest to separate when they are cold from the refrigerator; they beat best at room temperature.

1 cup sugar

2 cups dry red wine

1 vanilla bean

6 ripe pears, Bosc, Bartlett, or Anjou

PEARS POACHED IN RED WINE

This easy dessert can be served with ice cream, if you like, or sherbet, and mandelbrot or chocolate meringues.

1. In a saucepan or skillet large enough to hold the pear halves in one snug layer, combine the sugar and red wine. Slit the vanilla bean and add it to the liquid. Bring the liquid to boiling and simmer it while you prepare the pears.

2. Halve, peel, and core the pears. The peeling is done easily with a vegetable peeler. To core, follow the outline in the fruit with a paring knife and gently remove. Add the pears to the simmering liquid.

3. When the pear halves are tender, remove them with a slotted spoon to a serving bowl.

4. Boil the liquid until it's reduced to a syrup. Pour the syrup over the pear halves, cool, cover, and refrigerate until ready to eat.

AHEAD OF TIME NOTE:

In a covered container, the pears will keep for a week or so in the refrigerator.

PAREVE PASSION

This mousse is another of Bonnie Maslin's excellent chocolate desserts (see Tantalizing Torte, page 261). It's really much better than its title: it's rich and seductive.

4 ounces unsweetened chocolate (see Note)
¾ cup sugar
5 eggs, separated
1 teaspoon vanilla extract

1. Melt the chocolate in the top of a double boiler with ½ cup of the sugar and ¼ cup of water. Heat over simmering water until the chocolate melts, stirring from time to time.

2. With the top of the double boiler still over simmering water, add the egg yolks, one at a time, beating well after each addition. This is easiest done with a hand-held electric beater, though you can, of course, use a whisk.

3. When the eggs have been incorporated, remove the pan from the heat. If you're in a hurry, replace the simmering water with ice water. Beat the chocolate mixture for a few minutes to cool it. Let it stand in ice water while you beat the egg whites.

4. Beat the egg whites until foamy. Gradually beat in the remaining ¼ cup of sugar; beat until the whites are stiff but not dry.

5. Stir about one-quarter of the beaten whites into the cool chocolate mixture. Fold in the remaining whites, quickly and decisively, making sure no white streaks remain. Turn the mixture into a decorative serving bowl and refrigerate it for several hours before serving.

NOTE:

This is not cloyingly sweet; if you and your family know you like things *really* sweet, substitute semisweet chocolate.

RHUBARB-GINGER COMPOTE

2 pounds rhubarb, sliced
  into ½-inch pieces
  (about 8 cups)
1½ cups sugar
½ cup ginger preserves
  Meringue Shells,
  optional (page 252)

Rhubarb, like daffodils, harbingers spring.

1. Cook the rhubarb with the sugar and 4 tablespoons of water over low heat in a covered saucepan until the rhubarb is tender, 10 to 15 minutes.

2. When the rhubarb has cooled a bit, stir in the preserves. Serve at room temperature or chilled, in meringue shells if you like, or with sliced fresh strawberries or frozen yogurt.

STRAWBERRIES IN STRAWBERRY SAUCE

2 quarts strawberries

¼ cup lemon juice

¼ cup sugar

This dessert is simplicity itself. You can eat it as is, you can top it with ice cream, you can top fruit salad with it, and you can serve it in Meringue Shells (page 252).

Pick over the berries and put the bruised and less than perfect ones in a food processor. Add the lemon juice and sugar. Process to a sauce. Pour the sauce over the whole berries and serve. This is best served the day it's made.

STRAWBERRY MERINGUES

FOR THE MERINGUES:

6 egg whites

⅛ teaspoon cream of tartar

¾ cup sugar

¾ cup confectioners' sugar

½ teaspoon vanilla extract

FOR THE
STRAWBERRIES:

1 quart strawberries,
washed and stemmed

2 tablespoons lemon juice

¼ cup sugar

This summer dessert is not as difficult to prepare as it looks, and it's an impressive presentation.

1. Preheat the oven to 200 or 225 degrees (as low as your oven will reliably go). Line two baking sheets with parchment paper or oil them lightly and dust with flour.

2. Beat the egg whites with the cream of tartar in a standing electric mixer on high speed. Gradually add the sugar and ¼ cup of the confectioners' sugar. When the mixture is thick and firm, remove it from the beater. Shake the remaining confectioners' sugar over the mixture and fold it in gently, along with the vanilla.

3. Put the meringue into a pastry bag fitted with a plain tube. Pipe out 4-inch rounds with slightly raised edges onto the baking sheets. Alternatively, create the cups with a tablespoon: scoop out a tablespoon of meringue onto the baking sheet and form a saucer shape with the back of the spoon.

4. Bake for 1½ hours. Turn off the heat and let the meringues sit in the oven until they are dry and crisp. Stored airtight, they will keep, in dry weather, for about 1 week.

5. Slice the strawberries and combine them with the lemon juice and sugar. Fill the meringue cups with the strawberries and serve.

STRAWBERRY
PUDDING

This summer dessert is delicious and beautiful; make it when strawberries are plentiful.

1 quart strawberries
½ cup sugar
5 tablespoons cornstarch
2 egg whites

1. Reserve a few of the best-looking berries for decoration (see Note). Wash, hull, and slice the rest. Bring 1 cup of water to boiling with ¼ cup of sugar. Add the sliced strawberries, lower the heat, and cook for 3 minutes.

2. Dilute the cornstarch with 5 or 6 tablespoons of cold water. Add the cornstarch to the strawberries, stirring until thick. The mixture should be thick enough just when the liquid boils. Cool.

3. Beat the egg whites with the remaining ¼ cup of sugar until thick. Fold them into the cooled strawberries. Turn the strawberries into a 1-quart serving dish and chill for 3 to 4 hours before serving, garnished with the reserved berries.

NOTE:

To decorate with whole berries, slice them lengthwise from the tip to the stem, leaving them attached at the stem. Fan them and arrange on top of the pudding.

SUMMER PUDDING

1 pint strawberries (about 10 ounces)

1 pint raspberries (about 10 ounces)

½ cup sugar

13 slices sandwich bread or leftover challah, sliced ½ inch thick

Heavy cream, whipped (optional)

When made with local fresh berries, this pudding makes you glad we have summer. When made with frozen berries, it makes you glad you have a freezer.

1. Cut the strawberries into pieces roughly the size of the raspberries. Put all the berries in a heavy pot with the sugar. Over medium heat, bring the berries to a simmer and cook until they are softened and give off their juices — 2 to 3 minutes. Mash them against the pot with a potato masher, to achieve a chunky texture.

2. Remove the crusts and cut the bread to fit a 9-inch square cake pan that is 1½ inches deep. First cut the slices so they are the same height as the pan. Line the sides. Pave the bottom of the pan with the remaining rectangular pieces, cutting them to fit the curve of the pan as you go. You'll need some small pieces to fill in as well. It's like doing a mosaic in which you create the pattern. This is the display side, as the pudding is inverted and turned out for serving.

3. Using a slotted spoon, carefully distribute the fruit over the bread. Leave the liquid behind — you will spoon it over the pudding at the end. Take care not to disturb your careful arrangement of bread.

4. When the fruit is evenly distributed over the bottom layer, cut additional bread to make a top layer.

5. Spoon the berry liquid carefully and evenly over the top of the pudding.

6. Cover the pudding with a piece of wax paper, place a plate or pan whose bottom covers the top of the pudding on top of the paper (anything smaller will create an uneven bottom on the pudding), and weight it with a couple of 14-ounce cans. Refrigerate for at least 8 hours, or overnight.

7. To serve: Run a knife around the edge of the pan and reverse the pan onto a platter. If the pudding doesn't fall out onto the platter, give a sharp downward gesture, as if to bang the platter and pan against the counter — but don't go that far. Decorate with whole berries or, if you like, whipped cream.

TANTALIZING
TORTE

Carla Mayer Glasser, the agent for this book and its god-mother, was worried that I didn't have enough chocolate desserts. She quickly called her friend Bonnie Maslin, who faxed over this delicious recipe along with Pareve Passion (page 255). Ms. Maslin, a psychotherapist and the author of *The Angry Marriage,* is an impressive cook. I changed the technique slightly, but the recipe is Ms. Maslin's.

8 eggs, separated

¾ cup sugar

4 ounces unsweetened chocolate, melted (see Note)

1 teaspoon vanilla extract

8 ounces walnuts, ground (see Note)

1. Preheat the oven to 350 degrees.

2. In a standing mixer on medium-high speed, beat the egg yolks with ½ cup of the sugar for 10 minutes; the mixture should be very thick and pale.

3. Add the melted chocolate, vanilla extract, and walnuts. Mix with a wooden spoon just to combine.

4. Beat the egg whites until foamy. Slowly add the remaining ¼ cup of sugar and beat until stiff but not dry.

5. Mix about one-fourth of the beaten whites into the yolk mixture. Fold in the remaining whites, quickly and decisively, until there are no white streaks.

6. Pour the batter into a 9-inch springform pan and bake in the preheated oven for 30 minutes, until the top is nicely browned and the torte is dry when tested with a toothpick or skewer. Cool on a rack and remove sides. Serve the torte the same day it's made.

NOTE:

You can melt the chocolate in a microwave. Put the wrapped pieces on a plate and microwave for 2 minutes. With a spatula, scrape the chocolate from its paper directly into the batter. Or carefully melt the chocolate in a saucepan over low heat, stirring.

The nuts should retain some crunch; don't grind to a complete powder.

DATE CAKE

1 tablespoon flavorless oil

1 cup brown sugar

2 eggs

1 teaspoon vanilla extract

Pinch of salt

¼ cup flour

½ teaspoon baking powder

1 cup chopped dried dates

1 cup chopped walnuts

This flavorful dessert is a cross between a cake and a pudding. It's firm and moist, and would be delicious with whipped cream.

1. Preheat the oven to 300 degrees. Lightly grease a 1-quart baking dish, about 8 inches in diameter and 2 inches deep.

2. Cream the sugar with the eggs. Add the vanilla extract and salt.

3. Sift together the flour and baking powder. Add to the sugar mixture along with the dates and walnuts. Mix well.

4. Transfer to the prepared pan and bake for about 1 hour. Let the cake cool before eating. It keeps well, at room temperature, covered, for a day or two.

MENUS

These menus are meant as a guide, perhaps as inspiration. I've used recipes included in the book, but you should include your favorites, too. When creating your own menus, try to achieve flavor and textural contrast and make sure the colors on the plate are pleasing. Simple recipes that are not in the book but would nonetheless enhance a meal are indicated here with an asterisk.

POULTRY

Gefilte Fish
Chicken Soup with Mandlen
Roast Chicken
Sautéed Spinach with Currants and Pine Nuts
Carrot Salad
Apricot Compote

♦

Cold Fried Fish
Spinach Soup
Roast Chicken
Fennel and Apple Salad
Baked Apples

♦

Cold Spinach Soup
Gravlax and Mustard Sauce
Chicken "Balabusta"
Beet and Green Bean Salad
Date Cake

♦

Leek and Potato Soup
Flounder and Salmon Terrine
Broiled Orange Duck
Braised Leeks and Potatoes
Green Salad*
Banana Sorbet

♦

Mushroom Soup
Chicken Fricassee
Roasted Potato "Fries"
Garlic Green Beans
Green Salad*
Dried Fruit Compote

◆

Deviled Eggs
Brined Turkey
Potato and Parsnip Kugel
Glazed Carrots and Parsley Roots
Rhubarb-Ginger Compote (spring)
Mediterranean Compote

◆

Chicken Soup with Potato Kneidlach
Broiled Butterflied Chicken
Jerusalem Kugel
(Just Plain) Green Beans
Grapefruit and Wine Mousse

◆

Cauliflower Soup
Casserole of Chicken and Rice
Sautéed Swiss Chard
Pears Poached in Red Wine

◆

Salt Cod in Tomato Sauce
Chicken Pie
Green Salad*
Dessert Couscous

◆

Spinach Soup
Chicken with Pomegranate, Nuts, and Rice
Sugar Snap Peas and Carrots
Chickpea Salad
Chiffon Cake

◆

Herring Salad
Chicken and Macaroni
Beet Puree
Green Salad*
Granny Smith Sorbet

◆

Salmon Gefilte Fish
Coq au Vin
Mashed Potatoes
Braised Leeks*
Strawberries in Strawberry Sauce

◆

Leeks Vinaigrette
Duck with Pomegranate and Walnut Sauce
Rice and Orzo
Broccoli Puree
Green Salad*
Coffee Sorbet

◆

Gravlax with Mustard Sauce
Roast Goose
Root Vegetable Puree
Caesar Salad*
Meringue Shells with Fruit Salad

◆

Iranian Meatball Soup
Rock Cornish Hens Stuffed with Bulgar
Sautéed Swiss Chard
Strawberry Meringues

◆

Chopped Liver
Piquant Chicken Gratin
Iranian Spinach and Green Herb Pie
Braised Leeks and Potatoes
Greenmarket Applesauce
Mandlebrot

◆

Chopped Egg and Onion
Chicken Paprikash
Rice and Chickpeas
(Just Plain) Green Beans
Jellyroll

◆

FOR SUMMER

Cold Spinach Soup
Cold Fried Fish
Chicken in Escabeche
Rice Salad
Green Beans in Tomato Sauce
Tantalizing Torte

◆

MEAT

Eggplant Salad
Barbecued Brisket
Kasha Varnishkes
Moroccan Salads
Baked Apples

◆

Leeks Vinaigrette
Braised Lamb Shoulder
Sautéed Wild Mushrooms
Beet and Apple Salad
Ginger-Lemon Sorbet

◆

Flounder and Salmon Terrine
New England Boiled Dinner
Fennel and Apple Salad
Pareve Passion

◆

Baked Herring
Calf's Tongue with Capers
Broccoli Puree
Carrot Pudding
Dessert Couscous

◆

Stuffed Grape Leaves
Fish Cakes
Pot Roast Braised in Vinegar
Kasha Varnishkes
Beet and Apple Salad
Fresh Fruit Salad
Mandlebrot

◆

Asparagus Soup
Fish Balls in Lemon Sauce
Beef Shepherd's Pie
Carrot Salad
Ginger-Lemon Sorbet

◆

Chicken Soup with Egg Kneidlach
Lamb Shanks
Boiled Potatoes with Parsley*
Cauliflower Pie
Green Salad*
Strawberry Pudding

◆

Sorrel-Stuffed Hard-Boiled Eggs
Choucroute Garni
(Just Plain) Green Beans
Baked Apples
Chocolate Meringues

◆

Chopped Egg and Onion
Braised Short Ribs
Garlic Green Beans
Mushroom-Barley Pilaf
Fresh Fruit Salad

◆

Fish Balls in Lemon Sauce
Stuffed Breast of Veal
Beet and Apple Salad
Strawberry Pudding

◆

Huevos Haminados
Lamb with Honey
Roasted Root Vegetables
Farfel
Beet and Green Bean Salad
Chiffon Cake

◆

Vegetarian Chopped Liver
Brisket in Red Wine
Potato Latkes
Grated Zucchini
Carrot Salad
Tantalizing Torte

◆

Asparagus Soup
Shabbat Couscous
Sautéed Spinach with Currants and Pine Nuts
Moroccan Salads
Rhubarb-Ginger Compote

◆

Halibut in Egg-Lemon Sauce
Winter Beef Stew
Sautéed Mushrooms
Mamaliga
Grapefruit and Wine Mousse

◆

Lentil Soup
Curried Meatballs
Boiled Rice*
(Just Plain) Green Beans
Fattoush
Granny Smith Sorbet

◆

Leek and Potato Soup
Meatballs with Piperade
Spinach-Stuffed Portobello Mushrooms
Lokshen Kugel (meat)
Ginger-Lemon Sorbet

◆

Fish Cakes
Lamb Tagine
Whole Cauliflower with Pine Nuts, Capers, and Vinegar
Orzo Salad
Apple-Honey Brown Betty

◆

Leek and Potato Soup
Sweet and Sour Tongue
Root Vegetable Puree
Couscous Salad
Banana Sorbet

◆

Split Pea Soup
Stuffed Cabbage
Potato, Turnip, and Broccoli Kugel
Sautéed Swiss Chard
Coleslaw
Coffee Sorbet

◆

Fresh Tomato Soup
Meatballs with Piperade
Celery Root and Potato Salad
Grated Zucchini
Strawberry Pudding

◆

MEATLESS MEALS

Vegetarian Chopped Liver
Baked Carp
Celery Root and Barley Soup
Stuffed Red Snapper
Carrots with Ginger and Cumin
Jellyroll

◆

Baked Herring
Braised Cod with Chickpeas
Spicy Sautéed Broccoli
Pareve Passion

◆

Cauliflower Soup
Fish Cocktail Uncle Louie
Spinach-Stuffed Portobello Mushrooms
Leeks Vinaigrette
Dairy Lokshen Kugel, 1 or 2
Apple-Honey Brown Betty

◆

Fresh Tomato Soup
Fish with Walnut Sauce
Sabbath Saffron Rice
Grated Zucchini
Summer Pudding

◆

Russian Salad
Choucroute of Fresh and Smoked Salmon
Salt and Pepper Noodle Kugel
Spicy Sautéed Broccoli
Mediterranean Compote

◆

Leek and Potato Soup
Striped Bass with Lentils
Whole Cauliflower with Pine Nuts, Capers, and Vinegar
Orange and Olive Salad
Carrots with Garlic and Ginger
Jellyroll

◆

Cauliflower Soup
Roasted Bluefish and Potato Casserole
Sweet and Sour Cabbage
Fennel Puree
Apple-Honey Brown Betty

◆

Asparagus Soup
Fish Cakes
Braised Leeks and Potatoes
Carrots with Ginger and Cumin
Coleslaw
Jellyroll

◆

Mushroom Soup
Roasted Bluefish and Potato Casserole
Warm Cabbage Slaw
Beet Puree
Granny Smith Sorbet

◆

VEGETARIAN MEALS

Eggplant Salad
Lentil Soup
Mushroom-Barley Pilaf
Whole Cauliflower with Pine Nuts, Capers, and Vinegar
Fattoush
Ginger-Lemon Sorbet

◆

Fresh Tomato Soup
Cauliflower Pie
Rice and Chickpeas
Beet and Green Bean Salad
Spinach-Stuffed Portobello Mushrooms
Date Cake

◆

Russian Salad
Iranian Spinach and Green Herb Pie
Sweet and Sour Cabbage
Beet and Green Bean Salad
Pareve Passion

◆

Asparagus Soup
Couscous Salad
Glazed Carrots and Parsley Roots
Braised Leeks and Potatoes
Sweet and Sour Cabbage
Dried Fruit Compote

◆

Nahit
Mushroom Soup
Jerusalem Kugel
Potato and Parsnip Kugel
Sugar Snap Peas and Carrots
Fennel Puree
Meringue Shells with Strawberries in Strawberry Sauce

◆

Celery Root and Barley Soup
Russian Salad
Spinach-Stuffed Portobello Mushrooms
Grated Zucchini
Green Beans in Tomato Sauce
Pears Poached in Red Wine

SELECTED
BIBLIOGRAPHY

Anderson, Jean. *The Food of Portugal*. New York: William Morrow, 1986.

Child, Julia. *The Way to Cook*. New York, Alfred A. Knopf, 1975.

Cooper, John. *Eat and Be Satisfied*. Northvale, N.J.: Jason Aronson, 1993.

Dayan, Rae. *For the Love of Cooking*. Brooklyn, N.Y.: The Sephardic Community Center, n.d.

Donin, Rabbi Hayim Halevy. *To Be a Jew*. New York: Basic Books, 1972.

Field, Michael. *Michael Field's Cooking School*. New York: M. Barrows, 1965.

Goldstein, Darra. *The Vegetarian Hearth*. New York: Harper-Collins, 1997.

Greenberg, Betty D., and Althea O. Silverman. *The Jewish Home Beautiful*. New York: The Women's League of the United Synagogue of America, 1941.

Greene, Bert. *Greene on Greens*. New York: Workman Publishing, 1984.

Hazan, Marcella. *Marcella Cucina*. New York: HarperCollins, 1997.

Heschel, Abraham Joshua. *The Sabbath*. New York: Noonday Press, 1975.

Holy Scriptures. Philadelphia: Jewish Publication Society, 1955.

Kafka, Barbara. *Roasting*. New York: William Morrow, 1995.

La Place, Viana. *Verdura*. New York: William Morrow, 1991.

Levy, Faye. *Faye Levy's International Jewish Cookbook*. New York: Warner Books, 1991.

Liebman, Malvina W. *Jewish Cookery from Boston to Baghdad*. Cold Spring, N.Y.: NightinGale Resources Books, 1975.

Machlin, Edda Servi. *The Classic Cuisine of the Italian Jews*. New York: Everest House, 1981.

Marks, Gil. *The World of Jewish Cooking*. New York: Simon and Schuster, 1996.

Marshall, Lydie. *A Passion for Potatoes*. New York: HarperPerennial, 1992.

Moryoussef, Viviane, and Nina Moryoussef. *La Cuisine Juive Marocaine*. Paris: Jacques Grancher, 1995.

Olney, Richard. *Simple French Food*. New York: Atheneum, 1974.

Reider, Freda. *The Hallah Book*. KTAV, 1987.

Roden, Claudia. *The Book of Jewish Food*. New York: Alfred A. Knopf, 1996.

Schwartz, Arthur. *Soup Suppers*. New York: HarperPerennial, 1994.

Schwartz, Oded. *In Search of Plenty*. London: Kyle Cathie Ltd., 1992.

The Settlement Cookbook. New York: Simon and Schuster, 1965.

Sokolov, Raymond. *The Jewish-American Kitchen*. New York: Stewart, Tabori and Chang, 1989.

Stavroulakis, Nicholas. *Cookbook of the Jews of Greece*. Port Jefferson, N.Y.: Cadmus Press, 1986.

Wiesel, Elie. *A Jew Today*. Translated from the French by Marion Wiesel. New York: Random House, 1978.